SERVICE IS NOT
A PRODUCT

THE EXPERT'S GUIDE TO
SELLING SERVICE
AGREEMENTS

JOE SIDEROWICZ

DEDICATION

This book is dedicated to everyone I've had the privilege of working with in the service industry. I would not be in a position to write this book if not for the sales and service people who made my efforts a success.

I was fortunate to have Joe and Irene for parents. They encouraged me to work hard and not set limits on what I could accomplish.

My home is my safe haven. Spending much of my career traveling, there was no greater experience than returning to my beloved sons, Joe and Ethan. I can't quantify how proud I am of what they've accomplished.

My greatest fortune is having a wife who was at my side through the many highs and lows of my career. She is far more than I have ever deserved. Tara, you are the love of my life.

TABLE OF CONTENTS

Introduction   VII

The Service Sales Career

Chapter 1   **The Job**   1
             My Name Is Joe and I'm a Service Sales Representative

Chapter 2   **The Service Sales Environment**   17
             Boiler Rooms to Boardrooms

Chapter 3   **Skills Required**   33
             Listen, Think, Speak

The Process

Chapter 4   **Prospecting**   67
             The Ponzi Scheme

Chapter 5   **Qualifying**   93
             The Holy Grail

Chapter 6   **Survey**   127
             See the Forest and the Trees

Chapter 7   **Offer**   143
             The Age of Enlightenment

Chapter 8   **Pricing**   167
             Don't Discount Its Importance

Chapter 9   **Proposal**   179
             Will You Be Mine?

Chapter 10   **Presentation**   193
             In Search of a Standing Ovation

Chapter 11   **Closing**   211
             Easier Done Than Said

Chapter 12   **Objection Handling**   227
             Hit Me With Your Best Shot

INTRODUCTION

More than one million sales professionals are actively involved in selling service agreements for technology-based products. For many it's a major source of income. In almost all cases it's the major source of profits for the companies they represent. Ironically most companies don't dedicate enough resources to service marketing. For those that do, there isn't a lot of industry information regarding levels of investment and expected returns. Therefore most firms measure success based on historical performance in lieu of quantitative market analysis. Far too many companies are satisfied with incremental sales growth in service markets that have yet to be developed.

Every product or system manufactured and installed eventually falters or fails. Current product designs that integrate electronics, software, and mechanical devices require repairs, retrofits, upgrades, and ongoing maintenance. The growing number of products and systems being integrated has created a new category of users with wide-ranging service needs. Product applications continue to grow, but for the most part service offerings remain the same. The gap continues to widen and most service providers have not adapted.

Businesses annually spend billions of dollars to keep their equipment operating. Forecasts for long-term growth are strong across most markets. In down economic cycles, users often postpone purchases of new equipment in favor of maintaining existing systems. Service revenue growth continues to be strong regardless of swings in the economy.

Most companies recognize service as a major business opportunity. Initially technicians were responsible for selling service. As products and systems became more complicated, product salespeople inherited the responsibility of selling service agreements. This strategy required adaptation as service and maintenance costs grew and purchasing channels became more sophisticated. This created the need for companies to add sales personnel dedicated, in many cases, solely to selling service agreements.

Companies utilizing dedicated resources have seen strong growth. They've enhanced their value by building large bases of renewable revenue. All have increased product sales by capturing business from their growing service customer bases. It's the proverbial win-win: More product sales generate more service sales. More service sales generate more product sales. Progressive firms have recognized they can grow their market shares by expanding their brands, and they can do that by offering services beyond their existing product markets. This is usually accomplished with less investment and risk than comes with developing new products.

Typically salespeople are not attracted to service sales. They perceive it as inferior to selling big-ticket products and systems. This attitude is pervasive within most sales organizations. Selling service is looked upon as an entry-level position and a stepping-stone to something else. This situation has created a huge void when it comes to skilled service sales, marketing, and management personnel. It's rare to find individuals who have spent the majority of their careers in service sales or service marketing roles. Is it for lack of career growth? Is it due to limits on their earnings? Is there a shortage of experienced mentors? Do companies overlook salespeople and place operations personnel in key management positions? Is management tasked with growing product and service sales under one umbrella? I believe the answer to all of these questions is yes, even in companies with the best intentions.

Individuals with the skills to train and develop service salespeople are limited. Most companies utilize the same resources to train both service-sales and product-sales personnel. The information presented is typically generic in nature, falling short of what's needed. People selling products are trained to sell features, functions, and benefits. Service salespeople need to be trained to sell value and to master abstract selling concepts. There is little commonality between the two sales processes, and most companies struggle to adapt. It's not surprising service sales representatives have the highest attrition rates of all sales positions. They typically lack the proper training and resources to succeed.

Joe Siderowicz has more than twenty-five years of experience in service marketing. He has interviewed, hired, trained, or mentored more than 5,000 service salespeople. He is a recognized leader in his field, having built and led multiple worldwide service organizations.

Mr. Siderowicz has held executive sales, marketing, and general management positions with the industry-leading companies Honeywell and Simplex. He is the founder and president of the AfterMarket Consulting Group, which advises companies on how to grow service revenue. His extensive client list includes Fortune 100 firms and independent companies both large and small.

Service Is Not a Product: The Expert's Guide to Selling Service Agreements will describe to new and experienced sales, marketing, and management people the keys to success for selling service on technology-based products and systems. Personnel indirectly involved in service sales, such as technicians, engineers, administrative assistants, and others who work with customers, will also find the book beneficial. Readers will learn the unique skills and methodologies required to be successful from the industry expert.

Chapter 1

THE JOB
MY NAME IS JOE AND I'M A SERVICE SALES REPRESENTATIVE

I finally exchanged my hand-me-down, fire-engine-red, white-vinyl-topped, embarrassed-to-be-seen-in Plymouth Volare for a new company car. I had recently deposited my first five-figure bonus check. After living with my sister far too long, I moved into an apartment complex that was home to a group of sports and media celebrities. Leveraging my newfound confidence, I persuaded the admissions officer at the University of Pennsylvania to accept me into the Wharton School for postgraduate studies. I had received national recognition as a top performer and been awarded a trip to Palm Springs. My ego reached an oversized proportion when my boss told me, in front of my peers, I had to work only four and a half good days a week, meaning I could take Friday afternoons off because of my sales success. My ship had come in; I was riding a wave of success, But there was a problem—one that would trouble me for years. It didn't cease until I started helping others.

I just couldn't kick it. It would surface at the oddest times—during my morning shave, while driving down the White Horse Pike, or while listening to my coworker ramble on about his three-year-old son's future as an Olympic medalist. Although these encounters were brief, they were uncomfortable. The worst outbreaks usually took place in public places away from work. Typically I would receive some warning of an impending occurrence. I could sense it coming after the music stopped, after food was served, or when idle banter ended. Most often it came point-blank.

"Where do you work?" This would cause my brain to swim and my palms to sweat, and would trigger the typical symptoms associated with anxiety attacks. How could such an innocent question generate such ill feelings? I would go into evasive action:

"Hey, what do you think of those Phillies?"

"Did you hear the new one from Fleetwood Mac?"

Occasionally my not-too-smooth redirects worked, but for the persistent folks, I was forced to convey my version of the truth: "I sell computers." Only about one percent of my sales were software-based products, but desperate times required desperate measures. Early on I gave up trying to explain a job that usually brought looks of confusion, disappointment, or, worst of all, sympathy. How could something so good make me feel so bad? Over the years I came to understand I wasn't alone with my problem.

In reality I was a service sales representative for Honeywell. I sold repairs, retrofits, and maintenance agreements for temperature-control systems for heating and air-conditioning equipment for one of the country's largest corporations. I called on companies big and small, typically arriving via the back door or loading dock, as was the norm in the HVAC world. My territory included southern New Jersey's Camden, Trenton, and Atlantic City. I recall how, shortly after I took the position, all three cities were declared "economically dead" by a government agency. Another large part of my area was aptly named the Pine Barrens. Picture the Iraqi desert landscape filled with the Christmas trees no one wanted to buy because they were too ugly.

Urban sprawl—generated by the people who crossed the bridges to escape Pennsylvania's high housing costs and thousands of acres of farms that gave the Garden State its tagline—filled in the spaces in the rest of my territory. From my perspective it was close to nirvana. It was an opportunity to move to a new place, see new things, and meet new people. I still enjoy driving down unfamiliar roads and exploring new places. This enjoyment came from years of Sunday outings with my parents, who thought nothing of driving a few hundred miles to see a covered bridge or explore a college campus. Somehow we always made it back in time to watch the latest episode of *Mission: Impossible*. It was the best way to spend time together for a family wherein both parents worked long hours to provide for their children. In my case I was the youngest child; I have two sisters, Michele and JoAnn. These were great times that expanded my horizons and my desire to explore.

Even though I was only separated from Philadelphia by the Delaware River, I was a long way from the sophisticated experiences enjoyed by my friends working in Philadelphia's Center City. On the job-glamour scale, selling *The Philadelphia Inquirer*, at a stoplight, rated slightly less exciting than what I was doing. Explaining how a hot-water reset system works, how an air dryer enhances the performance of a pneumatic control system, or why you should hear a hissing sound coming from your thermostat could quickly lead a normal conversation to a slab in the morgue. No doubt about it, it was boring stuff to anyone who didn't have a vinyl pocket protector as part of his or her wardrobe. If I did come across someone who was genuinely interested, I quickly separated myself from the boring dolt.

I should have been bragging about my situation. I had just achieved my annual quota in five months. I was the top salesperson in the region. I had great paychecks and the freedom granted a sales star. What I didn't have was pride in what I did. It didn't start out that way, but in a short time there was no escaping it.

The Problem

I felt great pride in working for a Fortune 100 company. I was not only the first person in my family to graduate college; I was also the first person in my circle to work for a company that was well known even in my small hometown of Dickson City, Pennsylvania. This suburban, one-time coal-mining town is adjacent to Scranton, the setting for the show *The Office*. By the way the set of *The Office* looks like an environment a service salesperson can relate to.

Honeywell had multiple commercials on the most-watched TV show, *60 Minutes*. It was well-known and I was proud to be a part of it. All of the people I worked with were professionals. My account list included some of the most prestigious and recognized institutions in the world, like Princeton University, McGraw-Hill, AT&T, and E.R. Squibb. Sure I had my share of sales calls in prisons, waste-treatment plants, and research centers where seeing a cow with a Plexiglas window exposing its stomach wasn't considered unusual, and where I was exposed to odors that contaminated my clothing, but I got used to it. Being a sales representative was fine, but I was a *service* sales representative. The problem was the word—*service*. If you look it up in the *Oxford English Dictionary* you will find forty-two definitions across four pages. Without searching through this multivolume behemoth, I'm fairly certain it's one of the largest entries. Conversely, there are seven definitions of the word *product*.

Unlike *product* or *system*, service is a word that means different things to different people. The word seems to redefine itself every decade or so. In the 1980's the most common use of the word was evolving—it appeared everywhere from gas stations to cable television. I believe an individual's perspective of the word service is primarily determined by his or her age. People live and experience service in their own times and places. Does a teen today have any idea a convenience mart was once known as a service station, minus the mart and including people who happily cleaned your windshield and checked your oil? Does your grandfather realize his waitress is actually a server, or when service is used in conversations regarding the Internet it refers to bars that don't serve alcohol? I think you get the point.

BORN	
Pre-1950	"John is in the service. He's stationed on Guam."
1950s	"Can I check your oil, sir?'
1960s	"When are you getting cable TV?"
1970s	"We have a service that does that."
1980s	"Let's do the drive through."
1990s	Texting, 3G, 4G, etc.

Although the word evolves, its overall perception by the general public seems to stay intact. Rather than think of service companies like IBM, HP, or Microsoft, people more often visualize Comcast, Verizon, or McDonald's. Most people, when hearing "service," typically have negative thoughts. They recall waiting for a repairman, receiving an incorrect invoice, or being put on hold for minutes on end. People in service jobs are known to mop up, wear funny hats, require tips, have bad attitudes, or live someplace in India. None of these issues applied to my position, but occasionally I had to don a hairnet or protective goggles to do a survey.

It's not surprising people form quick impressions when you tell them you sell service for a living. Trying to determine which of the forty-two definitions they have in mind seems hopeless at times. I tried to evade the problem by adding words like engineer or consultant to my title. Actually what worked best was morphing service sales representative into environmental controls consultant. I clearly recall my hairstylist giving me more respect with my newly created title. She had no idea what I did, but it sounded impressive. In retrospect I think she understood my plight as she was also in the service industry. She played up her own image as a *stylist* rather than being tagged as a barber.

Service, both in name and function, is still evolving. Companies have upgraded their service departments to impressive-sounding *technical centers* and *customer support groups*. Salespeople are selling *solutions* and *enhancements*. Call it what you will, but it's still service. Some system, device, machine, software, or product isn't working as it should and help is needed.

In recent years the term *service economy* has become commonplace. Countless articles and books tout its growth, outsourcing, or offshoring. It has become commonplace in headlines and news reports. One would think the word has reached fashionable status, but like many high-fashion items, this one is a knockoff. Little written about or referenced in the new service economy is about actual break and-fix service. It appears financial institutions, health-care, and fast food companies have purchased the service domain name. I doubt any companies in these industries have real service salespeople. These service companies take care of customers by providing wide-ranging products like IRAs, dental plans, or the latest derivation of the taco. I speak to companies in the service economy that repair or improve tangible products that, in many cases, the typical person doesn't even know exist. I once sold service agreements for VAV drives and PRVs. Admit it you have no clue what I'm talking about. I'd explain, but then you may doze off.

Career Choice? Not Really

I have personally interviewed, trained, managed, or mentored more than 5,000 service salespeople. In all honesty that's a conservative estimate. Never—not once—did I come across an individual who had set a career goal of becoming a service sales representative. Most people stumble into the position unknowingly, by mistake or in desperation. Take me for example. I was working in the warehouse of a department store in the King of Prussia mall when I received a call from an employment agency seeking to fill a sales engineer position. Even the recruiter doctored the title rather than explain what the position encompassed. Next thing I knew I had a job offer from Honeywell. I had no real idea what the position actually required, but I did know it beat unloading crates of shoes and sheets. It also offered me the opportunity to move out of my sister's extra room, which was welcomed by both of us.

I did pause when I realized I was required to move from Pennsylvania to New Jersey. I was proud of my Keystone State heritage and my blue–collar, Polish background. My perspective of New Jersey was seen through the windows of various Buicks as we passed through on our way to New York City. How is it possible that an industry that employs more than one million part-time and full-time people is so misunderstood and unattractive? Why don't people recognize service sales as a career option? I can't say for certain, but I think it has to do with a report card full of Cs.

Conflict

Service sales positions are ripe with conflict. There is conflict with customers, fellow employees, employers, and other individuals related to the job. To sell service successfully, conflict-resolution skills are a must. Often a service salesperson will be faced with resolving problems that have no resolutions. They know their values come in to question when they enforce company policies that may seem unfair or even punitive:

"I'm sorry, but your warranty doesn't cover that."

"You'll have to pay the shipping charge to return the defective part."

"That's just a glitch in the software. We're working on it."

If you're looking for smooth sailing, work on a cruise ship. A career in service sales is not for the faint of heart. Often the worst problems develop with fellow employees. Animosity between the people responsible for selling products and those servicing the products existed long before the other Civil War. Not that I'm biased, but product salespeople are idiots. They sell stuff at big discounts, make promises to customers that are impossible to keep, withhold important information, drive cars that are too fast, have teeth that are too white, and kick their dogs. I apologize for digressing and generalizing a bit. These are the rants of a person who has spent his whole career in service.

Companies have invested a great deal of time and money in trying to resolve the conflict between the service and sales departments. High-priced consultants like me are hired to improve the sales handoff to service once an installation is completed. Service departments are getting more involved in reviewing job requirements and estimates before sales makes presentations to customers. Companies have created cross-functional product-design teams. Many hope Six Sigma programs will fix the problem. These are all worthy efforts, but divine intervention may be the only solution for conflicts between the noble folk in service and those mavericks in sales.

Harmony between sales and service is elusive-but not impossible. Service people demand quality and serviceable products; product salespeople demand better bonus plans. (That was definitely a cheap shot.) But in reality, a small amount of stress in the relationship can be positive. Think of service people as Congress fighting for the rights of their constituencies. Visualize product salespeople as the members of the Senate looking down from their lofty position, detached from everyday society. A company executive plays the role of president. This individual is in a position to determine if the company is driven by product or service needs.

Unfortunately, many executives have chosen to fund the next super, unbelievable, must-have products rather than invest in their service infrastructures. New products are sexy. They generate good sound bites and they help executives get reelected by their boards of directors. The backgrounds of most company presidents and CEOs include finance, manufacturing, marketing, operations and even information systems. Rarely, about as often as I see a red Blue Jay—have I read about someone rising to the top position in a company due to his or her service sales experience.

Customers

Products and systems break, are misapplied, are vandalized, become obsolete, etc. Customers expect uninterrupted operation forever. There is a built-in contradiction in service sales. The majority of successful sales are due to the failure or the expected failure of products made by the *excellent* company employing the person selling service. Motors burn out, wires get shorted, controls loose calibration, dirt gets in smoke detectors, and software has bugs. The list of potential issues is limitless. Service is required to correct all of these problems. Sometimes the service is planned or can be minimized by aggressive maintenance programs. Other times the failure is unexpected and ill timed. People get inconvenienced, frustrated, angry, or even outraged by the problems *your* equipment has caused. They want it corrected now! They may have already heard complaints from their customers, employees, or bosses. They may have already made promises to resolve the issue to fend off complaints. Service salespeople often walk in to charged situations. Sometimes they are welcomed as saviors; more often they face the wrath of scorned customers.

I was once thrown out of a hospital—figuratively—because one of our technicians left a half-eaten tuna hoagie on a heating unit that carried its fish smell throughout the facility.

Somehow it was my fault. The client was livid because his staff and patients had to endure the horror of smelling tuna the whole day. Personally I think it was due to comments from patients who had regained their sense of smell after eating steamed vegetables and tasteless hospital food for extended periods.

There were also occasions on which people who were a little upset threw the F-bomb in my direction. "Where is you f****** technician?" was an all-too-common refrain. My personal favorite was the ever-popular "the f****** person who sold this to me in the first place told me it would work better than it does."

Angry people don't want to hear from or see a salesperson. They want someone who can fix their problem now! On the other hand, I recall receiving a bottle of wine because I was able to fix an air-conditioning system for an especially hot group of nurses at the local hospital just by adjusting the thermostat.

Customers have little empathy when they're given excuses or explanations, regardless of how honest or original they may be:

"I'm very sorry, sir, but due to the category-five hurricane and the accompanying lightning and catastrophic flooding we just experienced, our technician may be a little late."

"I apologize, Ms. Hostile, Johnnie would have been there an hour earlier, but his dialysis ran long."

Customers don't want to hear they don't have service agreements or your company requires a purchase order before you'll send someone. Gone are the days when customers *requested* service. In today's business world, service is on demand. Some people thrive in this environment of conflict and stress while others find the going too difficult and move on.

Conditions

If you're reading this book in your office, seated in a high-back leather chair, bathed in natural light, with only the sound from your Bose system, you are not a service salesperson. (Unless you're at home in surroundings that were paid for by income generated from a career in service sales, like I am.) If you are fortunate enough to have your own desk, window, or door, consider yourself spoiled. It's more likely you're located in a bullpen, a Dilbert-inspired cube, or a warehouse area. Many companies have gone to the virtual office or shared spaces. These poor nomads find themselves cruising Starbucks or juggling their laptops and Blackberry's in the front seats of their midsize cars—spaces they share with their families of six and their dogs.

A career in service sales is for the resourceful, not the pampered. In reality there isn't an absolute necessity for private office space. What is imperative is the opportunity to connect with peers and the individuals who perform the services you sell. Unfortunately that takes more than a high-speed connection. Success in all areas of sales requires motivation and affirmation. Technology can't replace the need to feel like you're part of a team. E-mail and conference calls are no substitutes for face-to-face rapport building. The failure to build a community to support newly hired service salespeople is very common. Service is a people business. I've never seen an organization improve its performance by isolating its people. Companies need to focus on this issue, or else high attrition rates will continue.

Personally I benefited from my windowless bullpen office at Honeywell. Actually it was a desk surrounded by other desks, much like the set of any movie or TV show depicting a newsroom. Without question it was intimidating and difficult to hone my phone skills with veterans in earshot. This situation was outweighed by my opportunity to listen and learn. In my case it was more learning what not to say as I eavesdropped on conversations that would all too often end in "no."

In service the early bird does catch the worm. Once technicians get going they're hard to connect with as they're faced with overstuffed schedules. I made a special effort to start my day early and catch technicians loading up their vehicles with materials. I wasn't an ambulance chaser, but all of those repair parts had to go somewhere. Many of my best leads came from interactions with technicians in our stockroom. We had a great staff. They were experts at what they did, full of useful information, and, most importantly, great people. They were always sources for leads and always supported me—as in covered my ass when I all too often made mistakes. Blogs and conference calls are poor replacements for break-room and parking-lot wisdom.

The physical working conditions for service salespeople are fairly consistent. Company and local staff size may vary, but the surroundings typically offer minimal comfort. So if you're looking for paneled doors and picturesque vistas, it's unlikely you'll find them in the traditional service sales markets. If you haven't crossed at least two sets of railroad tracks to get to your office, your company is probably paying too much rent.

If you're looking for sophisticated surroundings and ambiance, seek a position in the financial world. If you long to work in a posh office tower downtown with an in-house fitness center and a coffee bar, look elsewhere. Welcome to the world of industrial parks, fringe neighborhoods, and warehouse areas.

Creativity

Something most service sales positions offer is the chance to be creative. Unlike product salespeople who are often bound by specifications, service salespeople are not as limited. In service sales you can offer customers as much as your company can profitably deliver. It's far easier to meet customer requirements for response times, scheduling, documentation, or service levels than to alter a product's physical characteristics or functionality. If your company doesn't offer the ability to customize your services, that's a whole other problem—a big one.

Over the years I've spoken and ridden with countless service salespeople. I've met with branch managers, sales managers, owners, vice presidents, and a few self-proclaimed dictators. One of the most common questions is, "Can I sell _____ service"? Or, "Why don't we sell _____ service?" The answer is fairly obvious: Can you deliver it? One of the great aspects of service marketing is the minimal investment needed to expand your service offerings. It may require hiring additional technical manpower, inventorying parts, or developing a new sales aid, but it's far easier than designing and manufacturing a new product. Selling service is a dynamic and creative process. Unfortunately some people aren't comfortable with this type of selling. They prefer taking their customers for test rides, performing demos, or working tediously with design engineers to meet project specifications. They struggle with discussing abstract solutions. Many need the coziness and comfort of great products, competitive pricing, preferred vendor status, or glossy brochures. What a bunch of babies.

Captive Market

If Maslow had developed a hierarchy of needs for businesses, service would probably be in the "basic needs" mix along with employees, customers, and profit. Companies can't generate revenue if the equipment they use to support their businesses isn't working or the environments their employees work in are dysfunctional. They may cancel service agreements, cut back on their maintenance schedules, or push for price considerations in a down business cycle, but they still require service at some point in time. Some of my best years for both selling and operating service businesses have been in down economic cycles.

Companies are quick to cut or postpone investments for new capital expenditures. Cutting headcount is commonplace. Turning off the heat, hiring monks instead of fixing the copy machine, or performing surgery without X-rays or MRIs isn't the norm. Even in dramatic situations when companies vacate facilities, they must inspect the fire alarm system, provide enough heat so the pipes don't freeze, and keep the roofs from leaking. Chances are the services you're selling are a necessity to some segment of the marketplace.

In my first full year of selling, I closed more than one hundred sales. It doesn't sound like much, but the previous national mark had been about half that. These were pretty impressive results for someone who was suffering from a severe case of career identity crisis. Almost all of my sales were unique in some way. In each there was something different in the offering, terms, application, or justification. I was never trained to approach the job this way. It was solely the outcome of taking the time and effort to closely examine the needs of my customers and create offerings with the best chances to sell.

It wasn't until I was in a national marketing position that I realized everyone else wasn't following the same process. Other people seemed to be trapped in the company culture rather than tapped in to the available market. This situation is still typical today in companies large and small. Service sales offerings all too often fall victim to company processes and procedures. They are company driven, not market driven.

People who spend significant amounts of time in the service sales industry hate to admit it, but it becomes part of their DNA. They really do care about their customers. They also treat people who work with their hands with the utmost respect. They're usually the first ones at their desks and are comfortable making sales calls from dawn to dusk. As managers they speak of "RMR" and "revenue streams" rather than big sales. But most importantly, they excel at relating to people and their problems.

Time spent as a service sales representative changes a person forever. I don't think there is a better sales position to develop your skills and gain insight into a diverse group of people and industries while generating a significant income and building a career in an area of sales and marketing that is still evolving.

Career Path

A career in service sales is a difficult road. The job is challenging, advancement is difficult, and the sales cycle can become repetitive and boring. Typically service sales positions are entry level and often used as a training ground for the development of product-sales personnel. Sales training is far too often on-the-job or recycled product-sales information. Even successful individuals who overachieve often face burnout.

Service sales positions traditionally have high turnover rates. People voluntarily leave the positions for better-paying jobs, for product-sales positions that may lead to promotions, or because they don't like the work. Many leave positions involuntarily. Some fail due to poor training or support. Some fail because they don't have the energy or drive required to do the job. Others simply don't have the skills or social style required and never should have been hired in the first place. Others just get tired of the long hours or their companies' inabilities to deliver what they sold.

Sales representatives become conflicted early on. They see their peers move on and begin to question themselves and their futures. It's not uncommon to be the office veteran after only spending a couple of years in a service sales position. Dealing with customer conflict is always challenging. Rivalry and conflict with other groups within a company wears many people down. Frustration or even depression may befall a service salesperson who feels his or her career progression is out of control.

With all that said, I consider myself fortunate to have built a career in this previously unchartered territory. I hope you find the information in this book informative and helpful in charting your own course for success.

Chapter 2

THE SERVICE SALES ENVIRONMENT
BOILER ROOMS TO BOARDROOMS

When speaking of a sales environment, I'm not addressing global warming. All sales positions bring with them unique sets of circumstances that affect day-to-day activities. They directly impact the sales representative's career development and sales performance and can be the determining factors between success and failure.

All salespeople work within their companies' internal structures as well as the markets in which they operate. Adapting to both of these environments is particularly difficult for new hires as they attempt to figure out where they fit in the overall scheme of things and how to meet their sales goals. Often a company's *culture* can be synonymous with its *environment* when describing this situation. Some environments can be stimulating, nurturing, or demanding. Others can be depressing, negative, or controlling. In almost all cases a sales representative is a product of his or her sales environment. For a service salesperson this is almost always the case.

Environments are shaped in many ways. I believe the two most important factors are people and policies. Both factors have a major impact on determining the overall performance of service sales representatives.

People

Management - Individual styles vary widely across the sales profession, but there are some traits that are most common. Most sales managers were once overachieving salespeople. They demonstrated abilities their companies felt could be applied to the development and management of others. Cloning comes to mind, as upper management typically selects people who bring in the numbers, often overlooking more important sales-management traits. I've attended many meetings where executives have discussed sales-management candidates as if they were looking for a stud horse, not a sales manager:

"We could use a hundred more just like Marisa."

"If Jena can generate these numbers in Pittsburgh, then we should be able to do it everywhere."

Typically management attempts to rationalize the selection of new sales managers utilizing multiple criteria. There may actually be guidelines issued by human resources. Regardless, it almost always comes down to: numbers=90 percent, other stuff=10 percent. And let us not forget the cozy relationship many sales manager wannabes forge with their superiors. Ever notice how your sales manager seems like a clone of his boss? I separate sales managers into two types: those who help you succeed and those who should be tolerated but ignored.

- o Helps You Succeed
    - Clearly defines expectations
    - Motivates you when you're second-guessing yourself
    - Respects you as a person and a professional
    - Listens to your ideas and suggestions
    - Is a mentor, not a master
    - Allows you flexibility to be creative and unique
    - Is a good person who happens to be your manager

- o Tolerated but Ignored
  - Is an arrogant, pretentious jerk
  - Says "this is what I would do" in most conversations
  - Micromanages
  - Doesn't know your significant other's name
  - Thinks putting you on the defensive is positive motivation
  - Uses the words *policy* and *rule* more than *guideline*
  - Schedules meetings or conference calls late on Friday afternoon

Operations - In my first service sales position, I was very fortunate to have a service manager who was skilled in explaining technical information to a dolt like me who glazed over whenever it became part of a conversation. Mike was a gifted engineer who explained technology in everyday language by leaving out details most engineers have the burning desire to share.

Mike could have easily penned the book *Technology Speak for Dummies*. I would explain situations to him, often leaving out critical information, and he would take out a pencil and create a simple flowchart I could understand and use as a guide to prepare my proposal. More importantly Mike enjoyed the challenges (my stupid questions) I would bring him. He had a helpful, supportive attitude not always present in busy operations personnel. He understood my sales were important to our branch and keeping his technicians employed was a noble cause. Mike also appreciated my ability to get top dollar for my projects, which allowed him to staff properly and look past the jobs I all too often underestimated and sold. Most importantly Mike was a good person.

I've had the opportunity to work with operations personnel in companies of all sizes. I've had face-to-face discussions with hundreds of service managers, supervisors, tech support specialists, engineers, and customer-service managers. I've been responsible for managing a staff of more than one hundred service managers and over 2,000 field-service personnel. I firmly believe the individuals who are responsible for managing, mentoring, scheduling, and dispatching technical resources perform the most difficult jobs in the service industry. Many are on call around the clock, most are understaffed, and all are responsible for meeting the exaggerated commitments of salespeople. Most find comfort in established processes and struggle when called upon to take on new challenges, especially from the sales side of the house. Their environment is extreme when you consider the stress levels brought on by the challenges they face every day.

And let's not overlook their abilities to get their jobs done while handling new product introductions, warranty issues, recalls, software problems, weather-related service spikes, technician turnover, headcount reductions, and implementing new back-office processes that typically fall on their shoulders. I was lucky to have Mike. I could have had Ike.

Ike is the service manager who is in the office at dawn and has three cups of coffee and maybe as many cigarettes before most salespeople hit the snooze button. He may have lost sleep responding to after-hour issues either on the job site or on the phone. Upon arriving at the office he first checks on problems that arose the previous night, then hopes none of his staff calls in sick, deals with missing parts that should have arrived two days ago, evades sales representatives following him around so he can shed some light on their projects, holds the hand of a frustrated dispatcher, calls a towing service to pick up a broken van on the side of the highway, answers countless e-mails, and justifies again to his boss why he isn't overstaffed. All of this typically takes place before noon. If he's lucky he may sneak out for a sandwich, but often another cup of coffee will have to suffice. The last thing Ike wants to do is sit down with a service salesperson and explain, for the tenth time, why lightning is not a good thing for his service department. By the way, Mike did all the above but always had time to support salespeople, especially a particular pain in the butt like me.

The relationship between sales and service is never ideal. In fact when conducting branch reviews, if the service manager voiced no concerns regarding the sales department and how they were selling him down the river, I was concerned. Either the service manager was soft, or he was told to take a vow of silence when meeting with the headquarter suits.

A healthy situation warrants a certain level of tension between the two departments. Salespeople need the sale and all too often overlook the labor or time required to perform the work. Service usually responds by suggesting more labor dollars be added to the project. Salespeople are quick to appeal to a higher authority, complaining service is pricing them out of the project. Typically service management is relegated to sit back and await a decision from upper management, as they are too busy to expend the time to defend their case.

And so the cycle continues as sales gets the order on their terms, and service meets their overzealous commitments and will ultimately face management to explain why their department's profit margins continue to fall. The outcome isn't surprising, as upper management tends to be more sympathetic to the sales perspective on most issues. I wonder if this has anything to do with the fact that most upper management has come from the sales ranks. It's a rare exception when the VP of sales and marketing has come from the service side of the business. I was one of those rare exceptions.

Peers - Much of who we are today is a result of the people we associated with over the years. Although they play major parts in this discussion, I'm excluding immediate family as I'm not a qualified psychiatrist, although I've played one on many a ride-along day with sales representatives. I'm speaking about the kid we rode the bus with in elementary school. The friend with whom we spent countless hours repeating, "What do you want to do?" and, "I don't know, what do you want to do?" The two people we hung out with in junior high because they met people's expectations of where we fit in the social order. The secret friend we had who was too weird to socialize with in public and the high school trendsetter we idolized from afar. Roommates, coworkers, internship acquaintances, romantic interests, bosses, and siblings all helped create who we are today. Good or bad.

The people you interact with in a sales environment play major roles in your perception of what is expected and how to behave. They give you the inside scoop on everyone, the spin on office politics, what not to say to your manager, how to attend your kid's soccer game without getting noticed, plus a myriad of other pieces of information that will affect your day-to-day performance. Experience tells me the first person who seeks you out to voice his or her opinions, perspectives, and whines should be evaded like an e-mail informing you about a large amount of money that awaits you in a Nigerian bank. Don't open up to this person; he or she will steal your identity and drain any energy and drive you have in your account. We all want to associate with winners. Sales winners are people who enjoy their jobs, perform at consistently high levels regardless of any barriers, and work hard to succeed every day. They leave whining to the underachievers.

The above observations apply to all sales positions. In most cases service sales representatives face even greater challenges. When everyone is responsible for selling service, the primary differences between one representative and another are usually tenure, territory, and sales performance. When salespeople are tasked primarily with selling service, the situation becomes more challenging, as they are typically in the minority. All too often management has minimal experience selling service. They are measured on putting big product sales numbers on the board. Most aspire to help service salespeople and will support them to the best of their ability. Unfortunately their superiors are typically pounding on them to deliver large revenue targets or they may find themselves back in the sales ranks. Worse are those managers who have some experience selling service and think they have it all figured out. They often draw on experiences that occurred in the distant past and are no longer relevant.

Not to get political, but equal rights for minorities is still a challenge for society. The treatment of dedicated service sales representatives in product-centric companies presents similar challenges. A good peer group can be hard to find for dedicated service sales representatives. If they are surrounded by people selling products or systems, they are all too often treated like second-class citizens from day one. New service sales representatives may hear comments that can de-motivate even the best people:

"Good luck! Our service is overpriced."

"If you do really well you can get a product-sales position."

"I don't think it's fair that I sell the system and you come along and get the commission for the service contract."

"I can't believe they've added another salesperson. My territory is already small."

This situation requires great care when hiring individuals to sell service. Great confidence and a "get out of my way" or an "in your face" attitude will come in handy.

Customers - One of the biggest differences between selling products or systems and service is the variety of people with whom you come into contact. Often people selling hardware are calling on clients of similar type, which I'll call a community. For example in the construction industry it's common for salespeople to cultivate a group of architects and engineers who can specify their product into a project. They can also build similar relationships with general or electrical contractors who have the abilities to select their product if they win the job.

Many of these salespeople rarely come into contact with the actual end users of their equipment. The building is designed; the general contractor wins the project and subs out the work to another company; the product-sales representative submits a bid; the sub selects the vendor that meets the specification; the system is installed; and then the building is turned over to the end user post-construction. In this scenario much time is spent preparing a competitive bid and gaining an edge with the installer. Time spent with the end user is minimal and often their identity is unknown.

The above example is a classic case that demonstrates why companies that don't have dedicated service sales representatives typically underachieve. In order to be successful, the above market situation requires sales representatives to have unique skill sets that relate to both purchasers and end users of their product or system. In most cases they are technically orientated individuals highly skilled in applying and integrating their products. Asking them to identify, qualify, present, and sell service offerings to end users may be wishful thinking.

Now let's address the end users of these products or systems. First you need to identify who owns the facility, then sort out who is responsible for its operation. Is it the owner or an outside firm? Is it tenant-managed or part of a chain? In the life safety world, a service sales representative trying to sell service agreements may have to call on a maintenance person, a condo board, a school superintendent, a property manager, a minister, a day-care operator, a hospital administrator, a hotel manager, and a plant engineer all in the same day! The titles and types of people are infinite. Before lunch you may find yourself sitting across from a Donald Trump lookalike. After lunch you're dealing with an individual who thinks butt cleavage is a fashion statement. You may spend many excruciating minutes listening to a maintenance supervisor explain why live bait is best or repress the urge to punch someone in the face as a purchasing agent goes line by line through your terms and conditions. It's all in a day's work when pursuing an order for a service agreement.

A salesperson selling service on medical equipment may call on a doctor, a nurse, a purchasing agent, an office manager, an engineer, an administrator, or a government agent to gain a service agreement. It may be as simple as walking in the door of a small medical group and meeting with the head doctor or as difficult as traversing the bureaucracy of a major research hospital in pursuit of the same $6,000 agreement.

We all know, through our own experiences, service is a people business. Regardless if that service is delivered face to face, over the phone, or via the Internet, people need to be pleased with the experience. That same axiom applies when selling service. I don't think there is any professional sales position that requires more skill and understanding of people than selling service. If you don't enjoy communicating and relating to your fellow planet dwellers, you have little chance of long-term success in selling service.

Processes

Established processes are essential to guide organizations through the maze of activities required to meet internal and external business requirements. I would be lying if I said I wasn't a process guy. No one who has spent his career in the service industry would have succeeded without recognizing processes are imperative to meeting customer requirements and running profitable businesses. That experience—along with my belief that spices should be placed in alphabetical order and ties should be color-coordinated on their respective racks— supports my case as a process zealot and organization freak.

In sales a good support system that includes processes that aid in sales productivity is important. Having procedures in place that simplify prospecting, pricing, proposal preparation, approvals, and order entry will go a long way in supporting a sales representative's performance. Typically the bigger the company, the more processes are needed to conduct business. It makes sense, as management of large, multinational corporations is complicated by their scale and the requirements of diverse cultures.

Unfortunately I've been involved with companies with only a handful of employees that have processes, most informal, that could rival a Fortune 100 company. Most often there is an owner or manager who does business in a structured way that has evolved over many years. In most cases he isn't aware of how his belief system and business perspective are his company's major barriers to success when marketing service. Even after making the decision to market service aggressively and acknowledging changes to his business model will be needed, he doesn't change. The same can be said for many larger companies.

Common Mistakes
- Productize service offerings to fit into current product or system sales structures, including pricing, proposal forms, compensation, order entry, etc.
- Require review and approval of every proposal delaying the service sales process.
- Unwilling to meet customer service requirements outside current sales strategies.
- Not eliminating barriers that may unsettle current sales and operations staff but interfere with the service sales process.
- Refuse to accept they have minimal experience or knowledge of current service marketing best practices, but think they do.

Companies that want to grow service revenue aggressively need to understand change is required in almost all cases. The needed changes may have minimal impact on the existing operation. For some companies the necessary adjustments are significant. They often require structural changes to organizations and addressing cultural biases regarding service. Often a great amount of effort and resources are expended on identifying and hiring people to sell service. All too often these individuals are placed in an environment that is not conducive to their success.

Gaining access to prospects, meeting ever-growing customer needs, competition, and meeting sales quotas are all challenges. Being frustrated and hindered by internal issues may make success unattainable. I often receive calls from service sales representatives who have attended one of my training courses. Many of these calls are out of frustration with their situations. By and large the most common themes are:

"Everyone was pumped up after your training, but nothing changed."

"I'm not allowed any flexibility on what I can offer my prospects."

"My manager is supportive, but we still haven't implemented..."

I estimate about half of the people who call me are gone within a few months. Soon after, I usually receive calls requesting training classes for their replacements. I'm the only winner in these cases.

Geography

Over my career I've gone far and wide to make service sales calls. I've made calls on four continents, in more than thirty countries, and in forty-nine states (sorry, Alaska), all with the intent of selling service agreements. I've traveled on trains, trams, trolleys, ferries, buses, subways, and helicopters. I've had elite status on every major airline at one time or another. I've been on planes hit by lightning three times, made two emergency landings, sat on planes for hours (five is my current record) waiting to take off, have prayed to every known god during bouts of severe turbulence, and have been held for interrogation by KGB agents in Russia, all in the name of getting a signature on a service agreement.

By and large traveling by car has been my most common mode of transportation. While driving I've hit a deer, almost killed myself on the New Jersey Turnpike while driving and reading the *Philadelphia Daily News*, stained my pants with donut glaze, coffee, cheesesteak, and other foods, and spilled countless peanut M&Ms on the floor while rushing to appointments. Oddly I've never received a speeding ticket.

Without any question the travel that put me at the greatest risk and generated the most near-death experiences was RWSSR, aka riding with a service sales representative. As part of my service sales training process, I would always spend a day traveling with each new person. Typically I would wait a month post-training to schedule the visit. This effort was extremely important as it allowed valuable windshield time to discuss the representative's progress, address any issues or concerns he was having in his location, and assess if he had a good grasp of our sales strategy. Just as important, the representatives departed the training class knowing I was going to appear at their doors in a month. This strategy motivated the new hires not to procrastinate, to make those intimidating first calls, and to get some proposals on the books before my arrival. I'm firmly convinced if I had not done these follow-up visits my service sales programs would have generated less than the expected results.

The travel was intense. It was not unusual for me to leave on Sunday night and return late on Friday night for months at a time. By the way this is not the recipe for a good marriage or parenting. I am very fortunate to have been blessed with the most loving and patient wife on the planet. She was both a mom and a pop to my sons on many occasions.

The logistics were typically the same. The service sales representative would pick me up at the airport or my hotel and we would be off for a day of sales calls. It didn't take me long to grasp the fact that these were no joy rides. I expected to hear various spins on why their managers were jerks, how they received no support in their offices, and how their territories were more competitive than everyone else's—and I was rarely disappointed.

I didn't expect my former students to drive like we were qualifying for the Daytona 500 or were traveling in an emergency vehicle. Apparently when management rides along, normal salespeople, quite simply, freak out. Fender benders, I recall three. Speeding tickets issued, at least a dozen. Close calls running red lights or pulling into an already occupied passing lane would require a number with an exponent. Obviously I survived these thrill rides, but they must have contributed to my early hair loss.

Many sales representatives are fortunate to have compact territories that allow for scheduling multiple calls timed with traffic ebbs and flows. Others need to develop schedules that allow them to group calls in remote locations. Typically the biggest differentiators are the products or systems distributed, the market segments served, and population density. Broader application means a larger prospect base. The main factor impacting the time spent covering a territory is typically the job description. Sales representatives who sell both products and services manage their territories much different from dedicated service sales representatives. These generalists typically call on service prospects in conjunction with scheduled product calls.

In almost all cases product sales take precedence, especially when times are good. Service sales calls are often sandwiched in as time allows, if at all. Obviously this limits the focus on service sales unless quotas and compensation plans reward both sales equally. This is rarely the situation.

Most companies justify travel with a common-sense approach. Is it worth traveling a hundred miles to make a product sales call valued at $50,000? Is it worth the same trip to sell a service agreement worth $5,000? On the surface the answer appears to be a no-brainer. But once you start to calculate the average length of a call, the number of calls needed to make the sale, the profit impact over the life of the sale, and metrics like qualifying rates and close rates, the story changes. I'll leave that discussion for another part of this book.

Geography does have an impact on service sales productivity. Quotas need to be set accordingly. Should a service sales representative selling service on elevators in midtown Manhattan have the same expectations as one selling in Valley City, North Dakota?

Places

To borrow from Dr. Seuss, "oh, the places you'll go" pretty much sums up a career in service sales. Having spent a large part of my career in environmental controls and life safety, I've done surveys and made calls in all types of facilities. They ran the gamut of commercial buildings: health-care, education, administrative, industrial, hospitality, military, religious, governmental, etc. More interesting were the locations within the facilities. I've done surveys in countless crawl spaces, electrical closets, boiler rooms, elevator shafts, freezers, labs, operating rooms, and rooftops that tested my fear of heights. I've walked the halls of cigarette smoke-filled offices in Tokyo, overcrowded hospitals in Moscow, animal laboratories used for product testing, cell blocks, and security centers in casinos. I made a presentation in a windowed conference room on the ninetieth floor that had my knees shaking and tested my fight-or-flight reaction. I've had clients that manufactured cars, books, pharmaceuticals, rubber bands, alcohol, food products, clothes, and countless other products that were fascinating to watch being made. A favorite was a high-end perfume manufacturer that had an employee factory outlet to which I had access. It made me look like a big spender during the holidays. I wish I had a chance to make a call on the people who make M&Ms.

Technology-based products are everywhere. Products and systems are installed in wide-ranging building types and locations. People selling service need to be prepared to enter spaces that are too hot, too cold, too small, too loud, too high, and just plain scary at times. Be prepared to bump various body parts, tear various articles of clothing, and sweat just about everywhere. If chemical smells, verbal abuse from inmates, blood, people crying out, spiders, or human or animal waste bothers you, service sales may not be the best career choice for you.

Chapter 3

SKILLS REQUIRED
LISTEN, THINK, SPEAK

I was preparing for a speaking engagement focused on the importance of hiring the right type of individual for service sales. On that particular day the right side of my brain was outpacing the tired left side, so creating the presentation was a struggle. Not surprisingly a distraction took over my train of thought. In this case the intruder rescued me from feeling guilty for my lack of accomplishment, but it also proved to be interesting.

While compiling a list of service sales representatives I'd been involved with over the years, I realized there were hundreds, and the task of recalling even a fraction of them was difficult. Forging ahead I decided to estimate the number to the best of my ability. I retraced my thirty-plus-year career in service marketing. I jotted down the companies I'd worked with, the programs I'd been part of building, and the people I'd trained. I listed the locations where I'd conducted interviews, the number of people I'd typically spoken with, and how many I hired or recommended to hire.

Utilizing the most conservative numbers I could muster, the final total was big—very big. My analysis revealed I had conducted over 4,000 interviews and been directly involved in hiring over 1,000 service sales representatives.

My next step was calculating the number of service sales calls I'd made. I started with my own sales experiences, added my post-training ride-along days with new hires, and the calls

I had made with struggling people and my national-account service sales representatives. This wasn't an easy exercise as the number started to reach a point well beyond my expectation. Was it possible to have been on over 10,000 service sales calls? In reality it was closer to 15,000, but that just seemed crazy, so I stopped counting. Regardless, it was clear I'd been involved with lots and lots and lots of service sales representatives and sales calls.

I take pride in having hired many star performers who went on to have great careers in service sales. Many went on to management positions in sales and marketing in Fortune 500 companies. Some started their own companies and became formidable competitors. An annual highlight was presenting sales awards, but more rewarding was the knowledge that these people were earning significant incomes—in almost all cases, more than they had ever earned before.

With that said my record for hiring service sales representatives who did not succeed was also a big number. Sourcing, evaluating, and hiring the right people for any position may be the most difficult challenge in running a business. The process is imperfect and dependent on many variables. Many companies have human resource departments that provide outstanding assistance. These departments are full of well-educated, highly trained individuals armed with the latest in hiring profiles, personality and skills assessment testing, and vetting systems that should yield the best candidates.

I was fortunate to have this great support on many occasions, but in reality my hiring experience suggests it's pretty much a crap shoot. This is particularly true when hiring service sales representatives as most companies, large and small, rely on people with little experience in marketing service to make the decisions. Does someone who has spent years selling products, systems, or nothing have the right insight to hire a service sales person? The answer to this question is clear to almost everyone:

no. But as a consultant one of the most common concerns I hear from clients is the lack of knowledge regarding what to look for when hiring a service sales representative. I didn't have a grasp of what I was looking for the first couple of years. I thought it would be easy. I just needed to find me—lots of me's. That didn't work out too well, as for most of my twenties I didn't know who me was.

Over time I developed my own criteria for seeking the best people. The first step was the realization that my goal was to hire only overachievers. Mediocrity was easy to come by and often difficult to resist when requisitions were not being filled in a timely manner. There was always a stream of resumes from people who had sales experience. My strategy shifted when I started focusing on and analyzing my overachievers. The same people were repeatedly winning the sales awards. What was their secret? Was it their territory, local management, previous experience, or the bluebirds that landed on their desks?

I overlooked individuals whose success was the result of being in the right place at the right time, and the one-year wonders. Often an individual's success could be attributed to the local office culture. Not only was the service salesperson doing well, but everyone at that location seemed to overachieve year after year. I drilled down into the sales numbers of each person. I believe metrics regarding activity and performance are very important in implementing, measuring, and managing a service-marketing program. The activity reports for under and overachievers were often similar. The major difference was the consistent quality of results common to the overachievers. These people had qualifying and close rates that exceeded the norm month after month.

Beyond the numbers their personality, intelligence and motivation traits also seemed to have similarities. Most of these people were outgoing, had strong value systems, and were bright, and, in almost all cases, they needed to improve their financial situations. Money is always a great motivator. Many were supporting growing families or looking to purchase homes or pay off college loans.

I never used any pretesting or phone screening before selecting candidates to interview. I focused on a close review of each resume. I would go through stacks of paper, pulling out the ones that looked interesting. Did they have outside business-to-business sales experience? How much experience did they have? What markets did they serve? Why were they looking for a new job? At that point I would narrow it down to a half dozen candidates and then schedule interviews. My objective was to select a few candidates who impressed me and would fit in with the local office culture. At that point I would turn the short list over to the local decision makers. They would schedule second interviews, check references, and make their selection. I rarely mandated a particular person be hired, knowing local ownership of the individual was critical to everyone's success.

In reality the hiring process was my first gig as a consultant. I would only prequalify the candidates. It was important for them to come back a few days later and interview with the local staff. This allowed the candidate time to prepare some good questions based on information they had received during their first interviews. Good questions are always solid indicators of a person's intelligence and energy. I don't think I ever hired anyone who didn't ask multiple questions during an interview. People with active minds always have questions. How could a person effectively qualify a sales prospect if she couldn't formulate good questions in her job interview?

Did I have a format for my interviews? Yes. Did I make some decisions based on appearance and demeanor? Yes. Were there days when I walked away with no qualified candidates? Yes, many. Did the local manager reject the best candidate and frustrate the heck out of me? Yes, too many times.

Typically I would get a good sense for the candidates within half an hour. I staged each interview the same way, utilizing very similar questions. I also developed my own shorthand that would help me classify and recall a person at a later date. If a candidate had any of the following notations in my notes, he would not join our team:

Talking Head

Words flow from these people like political commentators on Fox News. They are relentless and will be heard, like it or not. Oftentimes their statements have no relationship to the topic at hand. A simple question may result in a response that can stop time and have you wishing you were at the dentist. They tend to repeat themselves and run word counts that exceed legal limits.

A talking head not only likes the sound of his voice; it seems to propel him. At Simplex we had two brothers who were managers working in two different locations. They had the same habit of never pausing when they spoke. Both of them could drone on endlessly. The only way to make them stop was to interrupt, or they would continue full throttle. They were classic taking heads. I can only imagine what it was like at their kitchen table growing up, or sitting through one of their staff meetings.

Is excessive talking caused by anxiety, desperation, or just a prolonged stop at Starbucks? All I know is selling service is not a job for a talking head or a person with a case of diarrhea of the mouth.

Dating Game

These people conduct themselves as if they responded to matchups on eHarmony, not a job solicitation. They make you feel like you're on a first date, and their only objective is to sell you on a second date. They are warm, fuzzy, and all too often more concerned with making a friend than seeking a job. Typically their body language is casual, as if they were in a restaurant or a bar. They make a point of trying to get personal. They can turn almost any remark into an opportunity to connect with you:

"I noticed on your resume you were a baseball player in college."

"Yes. By the way I can get you tickets to see the Phillies and get you good seats."

"Why are you interested in our company?"

"I think we're a good match. We've both come through some difficult times and are looking for a new beginning."

Most service sales potential clients aren't looking for soul mates. A lot of people—me included—don't like being patronized.

Cover Girl/GQ Guy

They are dressed to kill, elegant, and graceful in every way. They could easily have come directly from a gig as a game show host or runway model. Their jewelry is exquisite and the quality of their accessories is enviable. Is that a Prada logo? The cut on that suit has to be Armani. Their hair and nails are perfect. Their skin is bronzed, often a little orange. They add class to the otherwise drab surroundings and make you feel like you need to go on a diet immediately.

I know if I passed them on for a second interview my local people would question my sanity. They will not fit into our service culture. They will turn off many potential clients and, more importantly, our technical staff may feel intimidated working with them. Often I pass on their resumes to the product-sales side of the company. They seem to thrive on appearance and not substance. Oops— cheap shot!

Needless to say, I hired many service sales representatives who were attractive, but they had to impress me with their intelligence, not their good looks.

Deal Maker

People don't understand them, so they say:

"I was the top person at my last company, but they let me go."

"Sure, I broke the rules a few times, but I got the deals."

They tell you what they can do for you and how lucky you are they responded to your job posting. They think they are the ultimate sales machines. It must be true as they were the top person at their last four companies. They seem to hold people who don't agree with their methods in contempt. Their goal is and always will be the next best thing.

The deal maker doesn't love sales; he loves manipulating people. His goal is very simple: make a sale at any cost. It doesn't matter if it's not profitable for the company; he makes promises that can't be kept or offers discounts on everything to everybody. Service is a very genuine business that requires honesty and integrity. There is no room for the disingenuous.

Van Gogh

There is still some debate regarding how the artist Vincent van Gogh lost his ear. Most believe his struggles with mental illness caused him to cut it off himself. Some believe his friend, fellow artist Paul Gauguin, did it. We'll never know. All I know is he had one less ear than the norm.

I've had the opportunity to interview many a candidate who had two ears, but apparently they were both inoperable. They could hear me but for some reason didn't understand me. I'd ask a question and their response would be inconsistent with the subject matter.

Question: "What motivates you to get out of bed and make sales calls on a cold, rainy day?"

Answer: "I make a point of going to bed right after Letterman's top ten list."

Question: "Why did you leave your last company?"

Answer: "I like to make all of my sales calls in the afternoon."

Needless to say listening skills are essential for people in sales. Service sales prospective customers don't easily reveal needed information. Dealing with them requires focus, understanding, and, in most cases, operable ears.

Pinball Wizard

Unfortunately real pinball machines are hard to find. I'm sure many people reading this book have never played one. To many pinball is just a computer game.

Pinball is a game where the goal is to score as many points as possible by letting a ball strike various objects while keeping it in play as long as possible. The only tools you have to keep the ball moving are flippers. Good machines generate lots of action, flashing lights, and sound. A pinball interview is very similar. The candidate jumps from one subject to another with no recognizable direction or intent. Questions and answers bounce around and are out of context.

These people seem to be operating in another realm. It's fast. It's furious. One minute they're talking about their last job and the next their divorce five years ago. A line of questions may include the compensation plan, parking, and if there's a sushi restaurant close by. The outcomes of these interviews are much like the old pinball machines: sometimes the flippers freeze and a ball just goes down the hole. Worst case you shake it too hard and it tilts—game over.

Action News

These town criers have the need to provide information. Sometimes it's specific to one subject, but often it's the full telecast. They may give you the traffic report from their trip to the interview; a descriptive overview of the weather that may also include an extended forecast; a report on the people they know who work for your company; and even a financial report on the industry. The brave may even wander onto dangerous ground and work in some political commentary.

One way or another they are determined to tell you everything they know, regardless of the fact that everything they say is common knowledge. Although these interviews can be informative, they always lack substance. It's possible there are potential customers who don't have access to a window or a computer and need news reports, but I think it's a very small market segment.

QVC

Before I learned how to delete all of the home shopping channels, I occasionally found myself sneaking a peak. I couldn't help but get mesmerized by the mind-numbing sales pitches. I always felt guilty watching, but I was free to do what I wanted in the privacy of my home.

Focusing on features and benefits is basic marketing. The home shopping channels figured this out immediately. If they only speak to the features and benefits repeatedly, over and over, multiple times, for minutes on end, and bore into people's minds, the people will succumb. Obviously it works as these channels are very successful and homes are filled with items that will never be used.

A QVC job candidate does the same thing. No matter what question is asked he will reply by selling himself. He believes he is the biggest and brightest, and in limited supply, and you need to act now to take advantage of this special opportunity. Ask him if he enjoys making cold calls and he will respond, "I was the top salesperson in my region and was first in my elementary school spelling bee." Ask him about his organizational skills and he may say, "I'm known as the database king and I haven't missed a day of work since nineteen ninety-eight." He's always selling and has little regard for you or the actual job. Buy me; you need me; and if you hire me today you also get a pasta measurer. I don't think a service sales strategy based on buying something so the salesperson will leave will work over the long haul.

Technical Guru

I saved the most common type—and my least favorite—for last: the tech talker. I've probably interviewed more of these individuals than all others combined. In many cases they were technicians who wanted to try sales. It made sense to them. They were *service* technicians. All that was needed was to change *technician* to *sales* and presto, they became service *sales* representatives.

Also common to this group are people who have successful track records selling products or systems. A person from this group usually finds his way to a service sales interview by doctoring his resume to give the impression selling service was very important in his previous position. Often it was, but typically he wasn't very good at it. A person like this usually responds to a service sales job posting with the assumption he is a slam dunk, as it's a step down, or else he has run out of job options.

Almost all tech gurus believe everyone enjoys talking about technical stuff. They often make technical jokes that are probably funny within their community but leave you blank, and in all honesty a little uncomfortable. They use words like *server port*, *sub array*, *portal*, and other terms that must mean something. They come to the interviews determined to impress you with their knowledge and grasp of technology. Many also look like the last time they were comfortable with themselves was probably—well, never.

My punishment for a guy like this was to give him an abstract question and watch him freak out. "If your prospect doesn't respond to your value proposition, how would you create a sense of trust and empathy that would affect the situation?"

Yes, it's cruel to treat a candidate in such a fashion, but a guy's got to have some fun. Besides, selling service requires a high level of abstract thinking. It's not about system specifications, what software upgrade 6.1 will address, or how cool a new programming tool is. It requires enlightening clients on concepts and ways to maximize their equipment's operation. Selling service requires selling value, not price. This is an almost impossible task for individuals who have high levels of technology testosterone.

Skill Set

Hiring people is serious business. Choosing the wrong person has repercussions for all involved. A misstep that puts a new hire in a position to fail doesn't serve anyone. Often it's not the result of hiring an unqualified candidate but of incorrectly choosing a person without the required skill set for the specific position. In some cases the person and the skill set are correct but the individual doesn't fit into the local business culture.

Such an experience may negatively impact the career of a good salesperson, and the loss of income may hurt her and her family in a major way. Unfortunately many of us have been in this situation, and it's not a nice place. From the hiring company's perspective, the impact usually has financial, personal, and strategic ramifications. The financial loss can be calculated by analyzing costs for hiring, training, salary, expenses, etc. The lost sales opportunities are impossible to calculate.

On a personal level the hiring manager, direct manager, and others in the decision chain share a sense of failure. To make the situation worse, there's always someone looking to point the finger at the person who hired that dud.

I think the most damaging impact is strategic. I've been called in to many situations where a company admittedly tried a service sales program, but it failed. Often the next step was to put the program on hold for months, even years. This all-too-common scenario is a real tragedy. The lost revenue opportunity isn't recoverable. The repercussions felt by the people directly or indirectly impacted by the failed attempt will linger for a long time. Skeptics will be born, naysayers will have their day, and the introduction of a new service marketing effort will be even harder to launch.

As mentioned previously I've hired a large number of service salespeople. I've hired many who failed. I've missed business and personal goals due to poor hiring decisions. At the same time I've learned a great deal from my experiences. After all of these years one would think I would be able to hire a star every time. That's certainly not the case.

Communication

The ability to communicate effectively with all types of individuals is at the top of the needed-skills list. Great communicators have innate senses for sizing up their audiences, whether it's one person or a group. They are confident but not cocky. They control but do not dominate a conversation. They are knowledgeable but not overbearing. They're honest, and clients believe they have their best interests in mind. They show empathy without coming across as disingenuous. They're creative and don't sound like they're working off a script or cross-examining a witness. They treat others like they would like to be treated and have respect for people from all walks of life.

Some people are born communicators; some master their skills over time; for others the struggle will continue. There are three forms of communication that need to be mastered to be an effective service salesperson: verbal, written, and physical.

Verbal: For some the spoken word comes effortlessly while others find it a daunting task. For many even the thought of public speaking can trigger an anxiety attack. Some people use a multitude of words and say little while others can make prophetic statements with only a few words. We've all been around people we wish would shut up and others who have us hanging on every word. There are those who make us feel like we have a communication problem as we struggle to understand what they are saying. I submit that in most cases these people are just rambling dolts who speak with the hope something they say may be worthwhile.

Obviously expertise in the art of the spoken word is a key to success in many careers besides selling service. At the same time a service sales position depends heavily on the ability to communicate abstract concepts, so it becomes imperative.

The variables that affect your ability to communicate with another person makes it extremely complicated: age, language, accent, ethnic background, location, time of day, etc. may all come into play. What we can't always determine in a short conversation is often more important: What's preoccupying the other person's thoughts? What is his experience regarding the subject matter you are addressing? How is his health, family life, or job situation?

It gets more complicated if you start to ponder how individuals behave when speaking to the opposite sex, the same sex, or a different race. We may think we've done a great job communicating while the person on the other end of the conversation thinks we're a complete jerk. One thing we know is there are many, many, types of people in this world. Many can be kind of weird or off-putting. Needless to say communicating is not a simple task.

We've all had days when we know we are not on top of our verbal game. I've had many conversations where I didn't even understand what I just said, but I hoped the other person figured it out. I strongly recommend that on those days when your brain and mouth are suffering from disconnect, play hooky and go to a movie.

I've participated in sales calls and listened to my protégés speak in such effective manners I could hardly contain myself. I wanted to interrupt in the middle and tell them how magnificent they were and how proud I was of their efforts. On the other hand I've been on calls where I had to cut in and prohibit them from opening their yaps again.

Role playing and public speaking can be helpful, but there is no better way to practice sales communication skills than just talking. It's one thing to roll things around in our heads. It's a totally different experience hearing our own voices. Oftentimes, when I'm conducting a training session, I actually find myself listening to myself. That may sound strange, but when you've conducted as many classes as I have you can find yourself operating on autopilot. I'm thankful I have this little voice in my head that gives me a swift kick when I'm not doing well. The little voice isn't perfect. It's the same one that tells me to eat a coconut donut when I'm not hungry and finish a book front to back even when I know it's terrible. Hopefully all inner voices have the latter capability, or you may not be reading this.

Written—Many people struggle with writer's block. I'm a great example of that problem, as it's taken me more than three years to finish this book. Much like verbal communication, putting thoughts down on paper or screen can be difficult. For many speaking comes more easily as you don't need to know when to use a colon or semicolon. When I'm addressing a group I don't have to stop and ponder if I should start a new paragraph or the proper spellings of *through* and *thorough*.

This is a huge relief for someone like me, as I'm a pitiful speller. I think it may have something to do with the questionable early learning technique my sister JoAnne used on me. Every Friday we had a spelling test in elementary school. It was my sister's job to review the words with me the night before. If I spelled a word correctly, no problem. Spell it wrong and she would hit me on the top of the head with my spelling book. Fortunately it was a skinny book, but it had a hard cover.

I can't imagine spelling skills have gotten any better since people like JoAnne (her name actually doesn't have an e on the end, but I've waited a long time for retribution) were replaced by spell check. The abbreviated version of the language that has developed for the purpose of texting doesn't help our written communication skills. I'm going to assume many of you reading this book have never sat down and written a long letter, in longhand, with a writing instrument that was not erasable. That exercise takes an extreme amount of concentration.

Almost all sales positions require some type of written correspondence. It's also common to generate proposals with a word-processing program. Many salespeople utilize the same e-mail or cover letter template over and over. There's no question technology has minimized the requirement for crafting great correspondence. Unfortunately most of it today looks like it came off the end of a conveyor built. It's sterile, lacking in creativity, and, in most cases, disregarded by readers.

Is this the result of information overload or just apathy? Either way great writing skill seems to be a lost art. What isn't lost is the need to communicate to potential customers your service offering and how it fits their specific needs. What's the point of meeting with clients, determining their needs, and then generating plain vanilla proposals? Even a simple three or four-sentence e-mail should require thought. Don't miss any opportunity to remind your clients what their needs are, what problems your service can address, and what makes you the right person to do business with. If everything is cut and pasted, you're selling your client and yourself short.

Physical—There are limits to what we can do to change our appearances. We have the options to lose a few pounds, change hairstyles, get a manicure, or alter our attire. Like it or not, people judge us based on how we look.

I'm glad I'm six feet tall, but being bald and ten—make that twenty—pounds overweight is my reality. Did my physical stature give me an advantage over others? Maybe. Did the lack of shampoo-commercial-quality hair limit my opportunities? It may have. In all honesty I doubt it, as most of my superiors, and many customers, were short and couldn't see the top of my head.

Most of us try to maximize our good stuff and hide the not so good. Can intelligence and personality outweigh the benefits of being mistaken for a mannequin or movie star? I hope so.

I believe the impressions we make on people when meeting for the first time are extremely important. These interactions are not to be taken lightly. If we make positive impressions, things usually proceed in a positive manner. A negative impression usually requires an uphill battle that is often lost before you utter your first sentence. Physical appearance, your handshake, eye contact, and the way you move across a room or settle into a chair all contribute to that first impression. People who lumber into a room, fall into a chair, and look past an individual when speaking will come across as suspect even if they're Penelope Cruz or Tom Cruise clones.

A man who first comments on the heat and then wipes down his brow or other damp body parts with a Starbucks napkin doesn't typically project a high level of trust. For some people, like me, projecting a cool, calm demeanor isn't always easy. I've hurried to too many calls and struggled to settle myself and cool down. I've sped up meetings knowing I had less than an hour to get to the airport. Who hasn't said "that's alright" when left waiting for a half hour for a client, knowing another call is scheduled in less than an hour? The ability to appear composed in sales situations is a valuable trait. It projects an air of confidence and professionalism.

I've been responsible for making dress-code decisions for businesses I've managed. The question still surfaces with many of my clients: what do you think our service salesperson should wear? Should he wear a tie or a company shirt? Should she wear slacks or a skirt? One school of thought says you should dress in a casual style to make your clients comfortable. The other contends an individual should look professional and wear a suit, tie, etc.

In service sales it's common for people to believe in the first school. They feel "dressing up" may intimidate clients. Not surprisingly many of these people come from operations backgrounds and feel most comfortable in casual attire. In actuality there may be situations when business attire may intimidate some clients or be challenging for the salesperson. It can be uncomfortable to be in a dress and heels while descending into the depths of a hot, poorly lit building for a survey or meeting. I know the discomfort of making sales calls in Phoenix in July while wearing a suit.

My response to this question is always the same: I'd rather be overdressed than underdressed. You can always ask to remove your jacket or carry a pair of flats to replace your heels. Walking into a room and finding your client in business attire while you're decked out in casual Friday threads doesn't give a positive impression.

People selling service need to project an air of confidence. In almost all cases the person selling service will not perform the service. The client is well aware of this situation. Regardless, the salesperson is the face of the company at that point in time. New clients rarely meet the technicians who will perform the work before purchasing a service agreement. They may perceive the only connection they will have with the service company is the person who sold them the agreement. If the service salesperson projects an image that is capable, confident, and trustworthy, it can only help gain more business.

Smart

Everyone is intelligent. Transcripts, test scores, certificates, and diplomas can, if necessary, prove it. Smart people don't have to prove anything. People who need to mention their various accomplishments or plaster their business cards with certifications and memberships in an effort to gain credibility are suspect in my book.

Oftentimes the word *smart* is used to describe an intelligent person. Personally I think there is a big difference between *intelligent* and *smart*. I know lots of intelligent people. I have watched them surpass me in many situations. I view intelligent people as those who have the ability to learn and comprehend at a high level. They were the ones in school who overachieved in the sciences and the arts. Whatever lesson was to be learned, they came out on top.

I've also known many intelligent service salespeople. They're always interesting to talk to and are often the most challenging students to train. They hold good conversations and ask good questions. Unfortunately some of the most intelligent people I've associated with did not make very good service sales representatives.

Smart people seem not only to be able to learn, but they seem better equipped to apply their knowledge. A word I associate with *smart* is *clever*. We've all heard the labels *book smart* and *street smart* applied to people. As for the skills required in selling service, my scale tips toward the street variety. Even average guys like me, given the right amount of time, can learn anything that is printed in a book. It may mean reading a chapter numerous times, rewriting my notes, memorization, or working with a more knowledgeable person, but I will figure it out.

As for the street smart part, that has always seemed to come to me naturally. My interpretation of street smart is a combination of common sense and awareness of what is going on in the immediate environment and in the society in which we live. Street smart people have a sense of what's going on between people's ears, including their own. They tend to have quick wits and, all too often, sharp tongues.

Street smart people enjoy observing and interacting with people at all levels of society. They listen closely and have little trouble quickly assessing discussions or social situations and how they can take advantage of them. This helps them turn confrontations into positive outcomes. A street smart person is not typically at a loss for words or outwitted. Either of these outcomes is a severe blow to such a person's self-esteem.

I'm not sure why some people are better schooled in street smart skills. It may be the environments they grew up in or people with whom they interacted. I consider myself to have some skills in this area. I think my son, Ethan, would agree as he's had some greats laughs at some of my quick retorts to rude and obnoxious people we've encountered over the years. I doubt this ability was acquired in my youth on the not-so-mean streets of Dickson City, Pennsylvania. I do think attending college and working in large cities have been contributing factors.

Most of all I think street smarts are a basic survival skill. I've never been the smartest, strongest, fastest, or best at anything. My compensation for this has been my ability to size up a situation quickly and figure out a way to use it to my benefit, whether it's a confrontation with an adversary, a relationship, an interview, or a sales call. I've talked my way out of intimidating situations on the schoolyard and in the boardroom. I'm not sure which one was the bigger challenge.

I don't have great insight into how to uncover this skill during an interview or brief meeting. I do know I've somehow been able to recognize it when interviewing candidates and make notations of "smart" on their resumes. This one word would usually move an individual to a second round of interviews. Often it's the ability and ease the person has in carrying on a conversation that makes it identifiable. Sometimes it's her ability to read the nuances in my questions or adjust her answers to my communication style. What such a person doesn't do is sound like a stiff—someone whose conversational skills seem scripted, overindulgent, humorless, boring, etc.

As mentioned in other areas in this book, outstanding communication skills are an absolute requirement when selling service. You can teach people the technical knowledge required to sell service on any product or system. You can't teach people how to think quickly on their feet in a selling situation.

Abstract Thinking

Selling service is often categorized as an abstract sell. I agree with this theory. I have not only sought out service salespeople with abstract thinking ability, but I made sure everyone was well versed on the concept at all management levels.

So what is abstract thinking? Here's my layman's explanation: It all comes down to left-side versus right-side brain usage. In this case *left* and *right* are not political positions but actual hemispheres of the cerebellum. The left-side enhances a person's ability to understand concepts without all the facts. Abstract thinking gives us the ability to analyze limited information and organize it into a complete picture. That may be the most simplistic interpretation of this complicated concept; if you don't understand what I'm describing you may come up short in the abstract thinking department.

When describing this concept to people I often refer to the art world. The most common usage of the word *abstract* is in *abstract art*. People usually understand what I'm speaking about when I draw a comparison between a work by Picasso and one by Leonardo da Vinci. They know Mona Lisa's smile is the center of much discussion, but at least she has a mouth properly positioned on an actual face, unlike some of Picasso's works, where facial features appear to be positioned randomly.

Abstract thinkers have an easier time seeing and appreciating the artistic expression in a Picasso, while most right-side thinkers see crap on canvas. Abstract thinkers tend to think holistically while analytical thinkers focus on the individual elements in a picture. Analytical thinkers need order. They tend to think in an A to Z process. Abstract thinkers are more flexible and have less problems working without structure.

When selling service one needs to be skilled in communicating concepts to clients. Unlike product salespeople, who have the benefit of technical specifications and performance data, service sales representatives often have to enlighten prospects about intangible services and maintenance concepts. In most cases service salespeople must educate their clients on the need to maintain equipment and reduce the risk of failure, the benefits of preventive maintenance, and the value of fast response when service is needed. They more or less are painting pictures with words.

At the same time they need to conduct sales calls that adapt to each client's needs and social style. I instruct my students to visualize blank canvases between them and their clients. They start painting the picture with each question they pose and each answer they receive. At the same time they need to adapt each painting so the client sees the complete picture. For some clients broad brush strokes will do. Others need a detailed view.

In the service industry there are more right-side thinkers in the client base, especially at the operational level. Most people responsible for the day-to-day operations of products and systems have some technical acumen. As for decisions makers found in other areas of an organization, there is a much more even distribution.

There are tests that can analyze and categorize how you think and your social style. Many companies use these tests for all sales candidates. For many others this is an expensive and time-consuming step in the interviewing process, so they forgo it. I didn't utilize testing when hiring service sales representatives, as I did with technical staff. In some cases we would test post-hiring, but never before.

Over time I developed my own test that became part of every interview. Obviously it did not provide any scientific evidence, but in reality it worked and continues to work.

Abstract Thinking Test—Approved by Joe

After the usual greetings and small talk I would give the candidate an overview of the position we were looking to fill. I would explain the role of a service sales representative and what we were looking to achieve. The description would be in general terms with key information missing on purpose. I would then proceed to discuss the individual's resume and work experience, and the usual mundane interview questions.

The test would come about a half hour into the interview. I would apologize and interrupt the conversation. I would convey that in my haste I may have given her an unsatisfactory description of the position. I asked if she wouldn't mind giving me her interpretation of the job so I could fill in any information I overlooked. The answer to this question would prove, in most cases, to be the deciding factor in determining if the interviewee had abstract thinking ability and if he or she remained a viable candidate.

The analytical thinkers would, sometimes verbatim, repeat almost exactly what I had said about the position. In many cases they would refer directly to their notes. They relied on the facts at hand. The abstract thinkers' responses were completely different, including their body language. They would reposition themselves in their chairs, collect their thoughts, and give me an overview of the position that was better than what I had provided. Their abstract thinking skills allowed them to fill in some of the missing information on their own. They were not only listening specifically to what I had said but were taking that information and creating a more holistic overview of the position.

Response—non-abstract thinker: "You said the position requires selling service agreements on your equipment in Barnes, Lackawanna, and Middlesex counties. The position requires working with your existing customers and new clients. It reports to the service manager and I would work closely with the technicians. It includes a salary plus incentive, and you're looking to fill it soon."

Response—abstract thinker: "It sounds like you're looking for someone who can take advantage of the opportunity to sell service agreements on the equipment your company and others have installed. I get a sense the individual you're looking to hire would need to work closely with your service and sales departments while at the same time look for opportunities on their own that would be good prospects for your service offering. Needless to say you're looking for someone who has good communication skills and the energy to do the necessary research to locate key decision makers."

Both individuals heard what I said. Clearly the abstract thinker was listening to what I was saying and at the same time visualizing the bigger picture. Which individual do you think would make a better service sales representative?

Organization Skills

Monitoring past and current installations, products approaching warranty expiration, contact information, proposals, bids, and other sales activity requires significant organizational skills. Some companies have sophisticated project-tracking and sales-management tools like Salesforce. com, which can make these tasks easier. Some salespeople invest in their own contact management software like ACT.

Regardless of the tools available, it ultimately falls upon the person responsible for selling service agreements to identify and contact clients in a timely manner. The complexity of installation schedules for the products or systems sold has a major impact on the degree of challenge. Identifying the actual installation date or usage levels that trigger a warranty on medical devices, office products, computers, or machinery is usually straightforward. When it comes to installing building control systems, elevators, or communication or integrated products or systems, things can become much more complicated. In many cases the installation is contracted out to one or more firms that make tracking the progress of the project challenging. Even after the installation appears to be complete, the actual date the warranty went into effect is often debatable. Did it start the date the installation was completed by the installer, when the product was commissioned by the manufacturer, when adjustments and bugs were worked out, or when the building received its certificate of occupancy from the local authority? Depending on which party you're speaking with, the answer to all of the above questions may be "yes" or "no." The end user typically attempts to postpone the date as long as possible.

Some people responsible for marketing service may be tracking dozens or even hundreds of projects concurrently. Needless to say organizational skills are essential so no projects fall through the cracks and the window of opportunity to propose a service agreement is not missed. Additionally there are proposals to prepare and follow up on, calls to be scheduled, surveys, estimates, meetings (both necessary and needless), and all of the other stuff that requires our time. Another area that requires solid organizational skills is prospecting. Since I will focus on that subject in its own chapter, I will only say having enough prospects in your pipeline to support your sales plan requires significant organizational skills.

I always provided and continue to provide service sales staff with tools to manage their activities. Long before everything was software-based I would supply call-planning calendars, proposal logs, and other forms that would help get people organized. These tools also provided some uniformity to our marketing and sales strategies as we were all working off the same forms.

Beyond managing activity these tools were designed to drive behavior. If we were focused on adding new accounts in a particular year, we would segregate activities in that area. The same would hold true for strategies to upgrade, reprice, or expand our presence in a particular market segment.

It would be convenient to say all service sales representatives I dealt with were well organized. Many put up big numbers year after year while disregarding my recommendations. Some had better systems; some had no systems. In the end it all came down to productivity. If they were overachieving I didn't care if they kept their information in their back pockets or frontal lobes. If they were underachieving the lack of organizational skills was usually a major contributor.

I think some people are inherently organized. I have no idea why I have the need to keep everything in its proper place. I find it hard to do it any other way. Even when I had over a thousand employees, my desk only had an in basket, an out basket, and a to-do list, as it does today. I pride myself on having never missed a deadline, a birthday, a meeting, and countless activities. I even have an "update to-do list" entry on my monthly to-do list. I still think the Palm Pilot was one of the greatest inventions of our time. Is there such a thing as being too organized? Any comments suggesting this are blasphemy!

Time Management

Time-management and organizational skills usually go hand in hand—the exception being too much time spent organizing and not enough selling. The subject of time management is covered in countless books and articles. Apparently it's an important topic or many authors, ironically, have wasted their time. Of course we all have too little time to do too many things. The proper balance between family, work, community, and personal time is almost impossible to accomplish. For starters what is the proper balance? With that said I will focus on the subject matter at hand: service sales.

As mentioned previously my branch manager at Honeywell and I had a special arrangement regarding time. If I continued to perform at a high level, he only required four and a half good days of work a week. He would let everyone know I was free to go home early on Friday afternoons. That was his way of using me to motivate the other salespeople. He expected me to be in the office on Fridays so he could enter the sales bullpen in the early afternoon and loudly ask, "Are you still here?" at an opportune time, when everyone was in earshot. There were many occasions when I wanted to remain there, but his expectation was otherwise. So off I went to a clandestine sales call that would give the impression I went home early.

In reality I was working six days a week. Unlike the other salespeople in my office who had families and balanced lives, I was single, and was, by default, driven to succeed. I would come in almost every Saturday morning and work until mid-afternoon. Sometimes I would also come in on a Sunday. I would use this time to prepare proposals, research files, and get organized for the coming week. It became habit forming as I quickly realized by having the office to myself I could accomplish far more in jeans, listening to Springsteen, than when the place was teeming with coworkers.

In today's environment many salespeople don't even have offices to go to. Technology has eliminated the need to sit in an office or be in the physical presence of other people. I can only imagine what I could have accomplished back then with today's technology. My goal was very simple: be in the field with prospects and customers during the week. I would do all of my paperwork on the weekend or at night. Maximizing my sales time had a significant impact on my performance. In my first service sales position I set some record-breaking numbers. Quickly I was known across the company as "the guy who sold a hundred jobs." The standard of performance up until my arrival had been about forty to fifty jobs a year. By the way, a "job" was service work on a building controls system. My success wasn't solely based on utilizing my time efficiently, but it was a major contributor.

I also made the effort to manage my territory—central and south New Jersey. My branch was centrally located, which allowed me to reach the extremes of my territory in about two hours. I always made sure when I went into a remote area to schedule multiple calls to fill up the day. Good planning also meant seeing the client closest to my home at the end of the day.

So there you have two key components of service sales time management: maximize your time with customers and limit non-productive time. It's easy to say but hard to do. Another area that differentiated me from my peers was *not* doing what was expected. For example the expectation of both management and salespeople was to present each proposal face to face. Another expectation was dropping everything for any request for a sales call. I never understood either of those concepts. I would see other salespeople changing their schedules, often upsetting already scheduled prospective clients, to fit in unscheduled calls or drive fifty miles to present small proposals. I don't know if they did this due to sales desperation or just some Pavlovian response. Hadn't they heard about FedEx or the telephone? Unfortunately there wasn't any e-mail in those days.

I would always respond, but why did it have to be in person? What's my ROI driving three hours and presenting a $1,200 proposal? Technology has made these choices easier in today's business environment, but in the '80s we were putting lots of miles on our company cars. The point being it's all about the numbers. Both your manager and you need to generate sales. Style points are good, but over achieving your quota is the name of the game.

Another area that made me a maverick was my prospecting philosophy. Why go after the small stuff? When measuring the actual time expended pursuing major versus minor potential prospects, it was apparent it didn't vary by much. The sales cycle may have been a little longer, but the reward was far greater. Regardless of the potential sale amount, you still had to locate the decision maker, make a first call, conduct a survey, complete an estimate, and make a presentation—the same sales steps, but the resultant sale would be far greater with the large client.

I don't recall a sales commandment that said all prospects must be treated the same, at least not in my book. It didn't take a genius to figure out "time is money" is high on the overachievers' commandment list. I also never let time hold me hostage. The best example was my quote log. Unlike others who would hold quotes open for months on end, I would clean out the dead dogs every month. I knew I had to make painful decisions when it was time to write off proposals and not be held captive by the false hopes an inflated quote backlog can bring. Sometimes I stumbled and slowed down my activity as I counted on the sure things in my backlog. Most often my projections were correct and the orders came, but there were far too many times when I deservingly hit some lulls when the orders didn't close and I had to rally. In short I was not valuing my time because I thought I had succeeded when in reality I had to work double time to catch up.

The Main Event: The Sales Call

What skills are required to conduct a successful sales call? A multitude of articles and books have been written on this single topic. Why? Well for starters it's an unnatural act. It's a mystery, drama, and comedy all rolled into the first act. It's a story that has a plot based on fact, fiction, and fantasy. Add an infinite number of characters, settings, and circumstances and trying to create the perfect script becomes impossible.

Let's start with the fact that most people hate being sold. Most of us immediately go into defensive mode when we know we are being sold anything. In my part of the country, the Northeast, we don't like being played. When was the last time you saw a salesperson in a movie or a TV show come across as professional or admirable? Salespeople are usually depicted as manipulative and superficial. I think the proverbial used-car salesman has tainted the waters for all of us who make a living in sales.

Regardless if the title is sales representative, sales director, sales executive, or sales consultant, people know why you're calling on them. You want to sell them something, and most of them think you're going to take advantage of them if they don't have their guards up. Why would anyone choose this profession? As you already know if you're reading this book, you probably didn't choose a sales career—it chose you. Almost all of us ended up in sales by default, and most of us are happy we did.

I've been on thousands of service sales calls and participated in countless role plays. I love them both. It's great to observe, but it's even better to conduct them. Don't get me wrong, I've made some calls that left me doubting my intelligence and purpose in life. I've ended in-person and phone sales calls considering a stint with the French Foreign Legion. That idea usually ended with the realization that I probably needed to speak French to do so.

Other times, when my performance was pitiful, I would seek solace in a few stiff drinks or a half gallon of mint chocolate chip ice cream, or seek out one of my friends whose life probably sucked worse than mine at the moment. So I'm going to keep this very simple. The basic skill set needed for a productive sales call.

- Listen

     Personally I have a hard time listening to people. Patience is not one of my strong points. It's always been that way. It's not that I don't care, but I think I've heard every question, objection, or form of small talk a thousand times. It's gotten to the point that within a few minutes I feel I can script the call—my part and the client's.

     Obviously this is not a positive attribute when you're a salesperson. The most important discipline I practice to this day is restraining from speaking at inopportune times. Sometimes I write on my notepad to remind me in simple words, "Shut up!" Almost all of my calls that fall short are due to not listening on my part. I have worked on this skill more than any other, but there is still a need for improvement. People want to be heard. They usually have relevant things to say, even when what they say is irrelevant. I'll leave you to figure out that comment—it's a little deep.

     Foremost you need to listen very closely to the client. Your next question should be directly related to what she just said. Too many times salespeople are thinking of their next questions rather than listening to what was just spoken. It usually goes something like this:

     "How is your day going, Ms. Bartoli?"

     "Well, I've had better ones."

     "Oh that's great. Would you like to buy a service contract?"

     "I may be interested, but I need to bail my son out of jail, file for unemployment, and have my left breast removed before I can decide."

"Terrific. I'll send you a proposal."

A little bit of an exaggeration, but you get the point. Sales calls are between real people with real lives and real responsibilities. Good salespeople are aware of this situation on every call. They treat people with respect and take the time to relate to the person on a human level before selling her something. In order for this to happen you need to listen closely to what people have to say—every single word.

I think it's almost as important to listen to you. In this case *you* is, once again, that little voice in your head that is listening very closely to what you're saying and providing live commentary. Hopefully your little voice is brutally honest and immediately lets you know when what you just said didn't make any sense. It's there to judge you and to coach you.

I'm not certain but I believe the little voice is somehow related to your conscience through marriage. I know my little voice has bailed me out on many occasions. Its only shortcoming is its tendency to label me as stupid, boring, or uncreative, but who am I to argue with the little voice?

- Think

One would believe we are always thinking, although many times our actions prove otherwise. Thinking comes in many forms. Some of us enjoy daydreaming, analyzing, retrospection, judging, etc. It can happen in quiet moments, while speaking, trying to fall asleep, or driving down the road.

When making a sales call, thinking needs to be focused on the present. Thought about the upcoming call needs to take place before the event occurs. This is something many salespeople take for granted. It's as if their focus begins when the call starts. Windshield time is lost listening to talk radio, music, or chatting with a friend right up until we sit down with the client. This time would be better spent analyzing the situation before us. Who is this person? What is her area of responsibility? How is her business doing? Who is responsible for influencing and making decisions? What is my game plan?

What transpires during the call is unpredictable. It's a dynamic situation that typically takes its own course regardless of the salesperson's plan. It requires analyzing the situation on the spot so any needed change in course can occur now and not later. Some people are gifted at thinking on their feet while others require time to shape their thoughts. For some it requires slowing down the conversation. For others open-ended questions or good follow-up questions can buy time to think. The solution can be as simple as more sleep or more caffeine in their systems to get their minds engaged. Whatever tactic works, it needs to be deployed to ensure our thoughts are focused and our minds are agile and able to take on any situation.

Thinking isn't like an after-party. It shouldn't occur the next morning. It needs to happen immediately. I strongly recommend analyzing all sales calls immediately after the call takes place, when thoughts are fresh. It requires stepping back from the call and looking at it in total. Did you accomplish your objectives? Do you have a clear understanding of the client and his needs? Will you be able to create the right proposal based on the information you have in your notes? It requires analyzing what took place but also an honest critique of your performance. If your tendency is to believe you did a great job but the client was a little weird, you've got a problem, because he probably thinks the exact opposite.

I have my own method for analyzing a call. It came to me while watching the late, great comedic actor Chris Farley in the movie *Black Sheep*. In one scene Farley is determined to deliver a pamphlet for his political-candidate brother to a lone house at the bottom of a very long, very steep hill. Shortly after Farley starts down the hill, he begins to tumble. He halts his progress after a long tumble by grabbing on to something, but again he starts rolling down the hill head over heels. His fall seems to go on forever until he finally reaches the bottom of the hill. At that point he dusts himself off, turns around, and looks back up where he came from, and utters the words I still draw upon after every sales call: "What in the hell was that all about?"

- Speak

    Our ability to communicate verbally is amazing. When you consider the number of words, multiple definitions, word combinations, accents, and cultural differences impact our ability to communicate effectively, it's incredible we are able to do it.

    Some of us need to speak while others prefer to listen. There are those who have voices that demand attention while others ramble on, having a negative impact. I'm not referring to communication skills in this section; I'm addressing speech. Not what we say but when we say it. Obviously common sense and good manners tell us not to speak over someone or interrupt a conversation. At the same time we may be in a situation where the clock is running out on a meeting and we don't have the information we need. That requires getting the conversation back on track without insulting the client.

    What a good salesperson can't do is just talk. By *talking* I mean opening one's orifice and just saying stuff—words that have no relevance to the task at hand, are out of context, or complicate the situation. Trust me, I've done all of these things and more.

The problem usually occurs when the mouth and the brain have a direct connection. Of course they're connected, but there needs to be a quick, intermediary stop. I'll call this the dispatch area. In the service industry the dispatcher is critical to the operation of the department. This individual typically interacts directly with customers and the technical staff to solve problems. This requires analyzing the situation and determining the proper response. Resolution may require dispatch immediately, the next day, or never as it can be resolved over the phone.

When it comes to speaking I think we need to operate like a dispatcher. When we have a thought and we feel the urge to speak, should we speak immediately, hold that thought for later, or let it pass? I believe a more effective passing game would probably help our overall performances.

Chapter 4

PROSPECTING
THE PONZI SCHEME

It's not uncommon for service sales professionals to devote more than fifty percent of their time to identifying and developing prospects for new sales. Needless to say prospecting is the first and foremost step in the sales cycle for service sales representatives. Many companies make serious efforts to train their people in the best methods and resources available to accomplish the task. Investments in prospecting tools like databases, mailing lists, and lead-generation programs are costly but considered necessary for many firms. Print and Web advertising and even yellow pages listings are common.

In some large companies the responsibility for prospecting has been delegated to sales associates, relieving sales representatives of the burden. These individuals place outgoing calls to various targeted groups with the goal of scheduling sales calls for their outside service sales people. Regardless of the arrangement, salespeople can't succeed without prospects.

Simply stated prospecting is the planned approach to identifying and creating opportunities for a sale. If you agree with this definition, you're overlooking an important goal in effective prospecting. If you believe any prospect is better than no prospects, you need to change your mindset.

Overachievers know the key word missing from the generic definition above is *best*. If you're not seeking out the absolute best prospects, you're wasting your time. The best prospects result in the best sales. Identifying and developing high-sales-potential prospects are a key goal for individuals and companies. To be the best, you have to work with the best. That applies to prospects, not just your peers.

I doubt anyone would disagree with the above paragraph, but most people also agree they should eat healthier and exercise more. Even with the best intentions in mind, you probably continue to pursue any hot lead that comes your way. It's a salesperson's nature to pursue all potential sales. It's hard to resist grabbing hold of a lead and selling it into submission. But the immediate gratification can come with a steep price. If you listen to yourself, there's usually a little voice in your head saying, "You'll be sorry" when a marginal prospect surfaces and you treat it like a hot one. Somehow, that little voice knows something you don't. It knows the price you pay for a sale might be too great. It might take too much time, be smaller than required to meet your goals, or distract you from implementing your prospecting strategy. The voice is probably speaking to you right now: "This book is stupid," or, "That's definitely something I do too often." Regardless of what it's saying, read on.

Prospecting Strategy

Service sales prospecting strategies come in all shapes and sizes. Depending on the company you work for and the markets you serve, your situation has its own unique criteria. Seeking clients who may need the services you sell is the common denominator. These unsuspecting people may not realize they need your company's service, but enlightening them to that fact is the fun part.

Most salespeople don't enjoy prospecting. Some think it's demeaning while others find it takes too much effort. Still others love the chase and set off like TV pathologists piecing together clues to solve the case. You know you need prospects. In fact you know you need lots of prospects—dozens, hundreds, baskets full of prospects. How do you find them?

Developing a prospecting strategy is easy. Doesn't your manager always nod in agreement when you review your usual list of prospecting ideas? Typically it's the last topic in your sales discussions as both you and your boss are running short on time and becoming bored with each other. Reviewing prospecting plans always leaves both parties feeling better, particularly after downer conversations regarding falling short of your sales plan again. Prospecting plans give people a warm, fuzzy feeling. Hope springs eternal as a long list of strategies and tactics are reviewed. Hope quickly morphs into joy as individual target accounts that offer incredible sales possibilities are identified. Both parties walk away feeling good. In most cases both parties have forgotten the conversation within hours, if not minutes.

There are various reasons for not reaching a sales goal. Usually sales skills, the economy, competition, company bureaucracy, and just bad luck find their way into the conversation. When is the last time you heard a manager say, "You're failing because your prospecting techniques stink"? Probably not quite those words, but you get the point.

Prospecting isn't a hotly contested topic in most companies. There's a tendency to utilize the same techniques over and over. I recall one sales manager telling me he hadn't changed the prospecting slide in his presentation in five years. Regardless of the strategy, the only person who can make you a top prospector is you.

Why Prospecting Plans Fail

- Plans don't get implemented because of distractions.

- Lack of ownership—the plan required by management is not initiated by the salesperson.

- The time, energy, and resources required to implement the plan are unrealistic.

- Fear your best prospects may reject you—and then you're a person with no prospects!

- People don't like rejection. Prospecting and rejection are synonymous.

- The prospecting strategy doesn't support the sales strategy.

Step One: Develop a Sales Strategy

It's not uncommon when asking sales representatives about their sales strategies to receive puzzled looks. Strange replies such as, "I want to be the top salesperson in my region" or, "I buy a lot of clients lunch" are also not uncommon. I would be surprised if twenty-five percent of service sales representatives actually have well-thought-out sales strategies. Far more people seem to know their companies' marketing plans. Few seem able to differentiate between the two distinct strategies.

In simplistic terms a marketing plan is painted with a broad brush while a sales strategy is more paint-by-numbers. It's portrait versus wallet size. The sales strategy is more personal and can be coauthored by the salesperson. The marketing strategy is required reading. At most company sales meetings, marketing people describe, in painful detail, their latest strategy and why it will guarantee success. Rarely is much time spent on reviewing the sales strategy.

At most meetings a sales manager follows the marketing presentation, voicing full support: "I'm excited about this new strategy," or, "I know my people are going to run with it and set sales records." This rah-rah speech is usually followed by enthusiastic applause or even a standing ovation. After the meeting salespeople gather in the corridor, eating cookies, brownies, or whatever else has been put out for grazing, and a feeling of euphoria sets in. Even passed-over-one-too-many-times-for-promotion cynics ultimately see the opportunity. Everyone heads home excited and a little bloated. Six weeks later, concern. Eight weeks later, fear. End of the quarter, panic!

Often a company's efforts to translate marketing strategies into sales strategies fall short. Even less effort is put into integrating prospecting plans and sales strategies. Sales representatives are expected to understand the vision and adjust accordingly. Unfortunately too many salespeople don't make the necessary adjustments in time to meet their goals. Some tweak their strategies while others take the plunge—minus the bungee.

Don't waste your time developing a prospecting plan if you don't know the fine points of the sales strategy. If your company hasn't clearly defined the strategy, it's up to you to do it. Service sales representatives need to know the expected average quote size, the average sale, and the number of sales required to achieve their goals. Where will the prospects come from and what is the specific offering and value proposition? How much time will be required for each step of the sales cycle? Which markets should be focused on? How will the territory be managed?

The availability of good information is important when developing a good prospecting strategy. Many large companies have databases full of important sales information. Unfortunately, all too often, the information captured is insufficient for meeting the needs of service salespeople. Too many databases and CRM systems are tailored to support product sales and lack the contact information for service sales follow-up. Others have timing issues that miss the best window of opportunity to pursue a service agreement.

If you work for a small company, you should be able to find the information in company records or by analyzing past activity. Bigger doesn't always mean better when it comes to information availability or service sales success. Many smaller companies offer better service sales opportunities than large, multinational corporations, which often supply too much data and not enough relevant information for their salespeople. Smaller companies are typically more agile, more responsive, and better in touch with local market conditions.

Service sales performance isn't always easy to measure. First, clear goals must be established as the basis for measurement. For some companies driving sales growth is the primary objective. For others service sales may be reduced to seeking incremental sales or even public relations. Additional consideration must be given to the amount of time that is dedicated to selling service. Generalists tend to be less productive than dedicated salespeople. Regardless of the situation the metrics that should be considered when measuring an individual or group performance are listed below.

Key Sales Metrics

- Lead quality—conversion rates of various prospect sources
- Appointment rate—the percentage of prospects contacted that agree to meetings
- Qualifying rate—the percentage of prospects that generate quality proposals
- Close rate—the percentage of proposals that become orders
- Average proposal size/average order size
- Metrics by customer type, service offering, and market segment

Once this information is in hand, you have the basis for developing important performance goals that will support your sales strategy and the development of an effective prospecting strategy.

Small performance improvements in any of these metrics can significantly impact an individual model. Typically, overachieving service sales representatives' metrics exceed the averages. Take care not to overestimate personal targets based on any single year's performance, especially one that exceeded your norms, good or bad. When in doubt, plan conservatively.

Quota/Average Sale = Sales Required
Sales Required/Close Rate = Proposals Required
Proposals/Qualifying Rate = Appointments Required
Prospects/Appointments = Prospects Required

As previously mentioned, I was fortunate to have broken some sales records. The only way I was able to reach this level of performance was by generating a large number of quality leads and efficiently turning them into orders. An incremental change in established prospecting methods wasn't enough to get me where I needed to be. What I needed to accomplish required a new prospecting model. I will give an overview of my model later in the chapter.

Suspect or Prospect?

In selling jargon a *suspect* is typically someone you think may be interested in your service. A *prospect* typically means someone you have qualified as interested. In service sales suspects tend to be places rather than people. Most service sales representatives have a fairly easy time identifying suspects by driving around their territories. Building size and usage often are the determining factors in technical service sales. Almost every facility has copy machines, a security system, a fire alarm system, heat, air conditioning, computers, etc. If it's more than two stories it probably has an elevator.

This is an area where service sales representatives have it all over product and system salespeople. A product salesperson is typically looking for new opportunities, which in many cases means new tenants or new construction. Nothing gets product salespeople more excited than seeing a crane next to a hole in the ground or a moving van in front of a building. If they're really hungry for excitement they can cruise engineering and architectural firms, hoping to get involved before the project goes public. Needless to say the competition for these prospects can be brutal.

In the exciting world of service sales, almost every building is a suspect. If it has equipment you can provide service on, it's fair game. It doesn't really matter if the building already has a service arrangement with another vendor. I've never met a prospect who was too happy with his current service. In reality I think it's easier to displace an existing vendor than to try to enlighten someone about the benefits of a new service agreement.

In service sales kudos are usually earned by taking business away from competitors. Far too many people get scared away when they hear a particular account already has a service provider. Seeing a competitor's service vehicle in a parking lot often creates a psychological barrier that's difficult to overcome. Personally I found great satisfaction and success in stealing competitors' accounts. It's ironic, but if you're not personally feared or even hated by your local competition, you're probably not going to overachieve in selling service.

Perfect Prospect

Prospecting is typically covered in most sales training programs. A great deal of time is spent identifying sources for suspects and leads. Good sales training programs also examine the best methods for contacting potential prospects. Typically, marketing communications tools like direct-mail flyers, brochures, e-mails, and effective letter writing are covered. Some companies invest wisely by training their salespeople on the use of telephone scripts. These tools are extremely important.

Rarely are service sales representatives successful without utilizing the resources their companies make available. Unfortunately many training programs don't fully educate their students on what makes a perfect prospect. Training staffs tend to focus too much attention on promoting current marketing strategies and generic sales strategies and not enough on prospecting strategies. I've had the opportunity to review numerous sales training programs for large companies. In almost all cases the subject of prospecting is glazed over and positioned as being common knowledge that doesn't require dialogue beyond reviewing some charts and lists. This shortcoming will negatively impact the performance of the individual and the company more than they both realize.

After three years of field sales, I was promoted to a coveted marketing position at my company's headquarters. My very first assignment was to develop a new training program. I quickly learned my recent ability to walk on water was in jeopardy. My boss must have been crazy! I had never trained anyone, had no clue how to develop a curriculum, and hadn't even mastered the art of the overhead projector.

In reality, though, it was the right business decision for my boss and me. It provided me with the opportunity to introduce myself to our widespread field organization as it required a two-month, cross-country road trip. I was fresh from the field, had developed a unique style, and had everyone's attention based on my recent performance. Hadn't I been the one whining about our inadequate, three-week training program?

Yes, that was me. Now I would play the role of defendant rather than accuser.

Getting started was a major wheel spin. I read books on sales and training. I visited our training center and reviewed the current material. I pitched some softballs at my boss, trying to judge what he was expecting, but he left me to answer my own questions. I was procrastinating and struggling to get engaged. I questioned my ability and readiness for this assignment and my new management position.

I don't remember when or how, but the answer finally came to me; build a training program that guaranteed success. That may sound like an obvious and lame statement, but it was what I needed to get myself going. It required throwing away all of the materials we had in place and creating a program that was more "how to" and less generic. It also meant conducting the training myself rather than leaving it in the hands of a training staff that hadn't been in the field or sold anything for years.

I continued this practice throughout my career. I always augmented any sales training by bringing in the best people from the field to conduct sections of the course. To be successful in my first real assignment I had to exploit my already-bloated ego and expose every tactic that worked for me. I needed to train people as if my life depended on their performances.

In reality, my life didn't depend on them, but my career did. I will forever remember my boss' comment: "When you're in the front of the room, you're the expert." I drew upon these words of wisdom in times of doubt on countless occasions.

For the most part, the existing prospecting subject matter was full of the same old stuff. There were lots of lists, reports, data, and call logs. There was a nice letter library and there were good call scripts. What I found lacking was a good perspective on what makes a good prospect. My company, like many others I've worked with in my consulting practice, had made a leap of faith and proceeded directly from prospecting to qualifying. The information presented taught people some good things; hence it produced *good* salespeople. It was time to upgrade to *great*.

Rather than having attendees sit through another two-hour prospecting discussion that would bore them into submission, I would make them teach each other. I also covered the topic first thing in the morning, before the lethargy meter rose too high. I began this section of my training with a group exercise. I asked the class to define the perfect prospect. Quickly a long list was developed that had every need, decision criteria, and economic and business issue known to man. Usually one bright student also figured out what we'd created was a big laundry list of stuff that was far from the perfection we were seeking. We didn't create the perfect prospect but some form of mutant.

We would then proceed into a more informative discussion, attempting to rationalize the intuitive process required of a good prospector. What makes a perfect prospect? An urgent service need? A big budget? An identified decision maker? Or a short sales cycle? Would you rather have a decision maker with no money or a sponsor with connections? Is it worth pursuing an unwilling prospect even when you know you're their only choice for service?

These discussions usually revealed to my students one of the most important impressions I wanted them to get from the training: all prospects are not created equal. Good prospects don't necessarily generate *great* sales. If you sell service you should take the time to consider what the perfect prospect is for your market segment. It will force you to analyze your successes and failures objectively. It will help you spend your time more effectively. Most important, it will minimize the occasions on which you drag a mediocre prospect down the aisle of the sales cycle.

Planning and Organization

Developing and managing multiple prospecting sources requires a significant amount of organizational skill. Every effort needs to be made to streamline the process to ensure you're in front of people who are interested in purchasing your service.

Prospecting can easily consume the majority of the overall sales time expended. There isn't any specific target for the correct amount of time that should be dedicated to this step in the sales cycle. Exceeding your assigned quota is always the goal. If you can consistently make that happen, the amount of time spent on prospecting is unimportant. If you're an underachiever, you need to examine the cause. Lack of great prospects is often a major contributor to failure.

One commonality of good prospectors is the organized way they approach the task. Typically they select two or three strategies and consistently work those resources. They tend to keep solid records, pay attention to details, and are always fearful that at some point in time the sales tap will dry out. In short their prospecting appetites are insatiable.

On the other hand, poor prospectors tend to work in short bursts motivated by their personal weather forecasts. Without fail a sales drought occurs and they hit the panic button. Poor prospectors show up in jeans early one morning with venti cappuccinos and renewed commitments to finding some leads. For some it's too late; their managers have grown weary of their inconsistency. Others survive another month, quarter, or year and repeat the process again and again.

I had the advantage of being organized and process driven. These two qualities and my desire to make some serious money made me a good prospector. I probably had a dozen different strategies up my sleeve but primarily concentrated on two at a time. Foremost was my Ponzi prospecting scheme. It was usually complemented by a second strategy driven by current market conditions. I don't ever recall having a shortage of solid leads. I do recall spending a significant amount of time working my plan.

I feel bad for people who only find motivation in the face of failure. They approach prospecting as some type of batch process. They don't see the problem created by shutting down their sales assembly line for a few days each month to fix the problem.

It's disruptive to their performance and rarely generates the quality leads required to overachieve.

Panic prospecting has a trickle-down effect. It impacts the way salespeople speak and present themselves to potential customers. It can make them seem pushy, and no one likes to deal with that. It can also affect the qualification process when service salespeople go into a meeting feeling desperate. This situation usually results in doing a subpar job that only adds injury to an already struggling representative.

It can also impact the quality of offerings, proposals, and, in the end, close rates. Not surprisingly the willingness to discount and make unnecessary concessions may come in to play when sales slowdown. Service sales success requires consistent performance. Attaining quotas that require large numbers of sales rarely happens if prospecting is not an ongoing priority.

Sources

Source availability and quality varies widely in service sales. Typically company size and markets served are the greatest variables. For some people working in smaller companies the local phone book is a vital resource. At the other extreme are large, multinational companies that supply their sales forces with comprehensive information from databases. It's impossible to address all industries and their associated specific nuances in this book. But here is a list of some of the primary prospecting resources commonly utilized in service sales.

Current customers: Having your company's product present in an account is always beneficial to a service salesperson. The opportunity to sell service or upgrades is much easier when your company has an existing relationship with a prospect. The ability to schedule an appointment and the effort required to qualify the prospect is typically easier.

Pros: These prospects are typically prequalified. It's up to the service salesperson to identify and present offerings that interest the customer.

Cons: The current level of service and customer satisfaction, high or low, may limit the opportunity for additional revenue. The implied requirement by most employers to pursue these accounts may actually distract a service sales representative from seeking more rewarding opportunities. In some cases the existing customer base may be best pursued by inside salespeople or on-site technical staff. Outside salespeople may be more productive when given a goal to grow market share by gaining new customers.

New product sales: If you work for a company that sells new equipment, you have the benefit of knowing the warranty parameters and following up with a timely service proposal. For many companies this is the most common source of prospects and is rarely overlooked. Companies typically have processes in place to pursue these opportunities. Some allow the product salesperson to pursue the service sale while others have created processes to hand off opportunities to service sales representative. I don't know of any situation in which the handoff process is foolproof and not a source of some frustration.

Pros: The customer requires service. Who is better to provide service than the company that sold them the product? If the handoff is smooth, competition is usually not a factor. Good information is available about the equipment and installation.

Cons: It's not unusual that the handoff process isn't functioning correctly. The product salesperson may be late or even resistant to providing information in a timely fashion. The product salesperson may have already discussed service options with the customer that contradict the service sales strategy. Service concessions made during the product sale or extended warranties already may have been agreed to. These are also some of the reasons why companies need dedicated service salespeople. Expecting product salespeople to maximize service sales opportunities is unrealistic. They typically don't have the training or the sense of urgency to make it happen.

Warranty list: Typically a customer is faced with making a service decision before warranty expiration. Providing the equipment has performed up to par, the customer is usually receptive to or even enthusiastic about purchasing a service agreement.

Pros: This group can't be overlooked. They typically offer the best opportunities for most service salespeople. They are identifiable, prequalified, and, if business is strong, readily available. With that said, locating the people who will make the service buying decisions may not be easy. They are quite often different from the individuals involved in the original equipment purchases.

Cons: Often the actual warranty expiration date is unclear and contested. This scenario is fairly typical and can significantly extend the sales cycle. In many service sales markets the service decision maker is not the original purchaser. The service salesperson may have to approach the account as if it were a suspect rather than a prospect. A thorough qualifying job is required. Timing is everything in maximizing the warranty opportunity. If you're pursuing these customers in the last quarter of their warranties, you may be too late. Taking in-warranty prospects for granted is not unusual.

Renewals: Most companies have some type of renewal process in place. Some are highly automated while some require sales or administrative involvement. Existing customers offer the best opportunities to sell upgrades and additional services. If the agreement is set up to renew automatically, there is little need for a service salesperson to be involved.

Pros: This group is easy to identify, and service records are available. A little research on a customer's service coverage and history can quickly uncover opportunities. Existing relationships between key individuals may be leveraged. Adding additional services to an existing agreement may bypass cumbersome purchasing procedures.

Cons: Presenting a service upgrade may delay the renewal. Customers who are displeased with their service performance may be motivated to source other vendors when made aware of impending renewals. Although this prospect group is attractive, pursuing it can easily distract a service salesperson from pursuing more rewarding business elsewhere.

Product owners/no service: Hopefully this is a short list for your company. These are the customers that have your equipment, are beyond the warranty period, and have chosen not to buy service agreements. They may purchase service on an as-needed basis, use a competitor, or perform their own service. This category of prospect presents significant opportunities if approached correctly. Take care not to lump these prospects together as a group but to view them as individual opportunities. Approach each with a well-thought-out strategy.

Pros: Equipment breaks and needs to be maintained or repaired. You should have a good idea of the service requirements based on the equipment installed, its age, and its application. On many occasions the situation or individual that prevented a customer from entering into a service relationship has changed. A cold prospect can be turned into a hot prospect given the proper sales strategy.

Cons: Often the information regarding this group is lost or out of date. People are quick to form opinions of these customers, often based on unreliable information:

"Don't call them—they hate us and the operations manager is a jerk."

"They're using El Cheapo service. They only buy based on price."

"They have a big staff that does their own service work."

Sometimes the information may be true and your effort may be wasted. It takes time to qualify these prospects, but they should be pursued, especially if they're larger accounts. I've heard every reason imaginable, including the ones just mentioned, why a potential customer shouldn't be pursued. In almost all cases the information was proven unreliable. Some of my largest sales came from this group of so-called bad prospects.

Cancelled contracts/lost sales: Customers cancel for many reasons. Sometimes situations are unavoidable as companies cut back on spending or choose pay-as-you-go arrangements. Even when poor service performance triggered a cancellation, the situation may have changed. Unless you're convinced your company delivers inferior service compared to the competition, this is a great source for leads. The same goes for lost product sales. Someone has to perform service even if your company didn't sell the equipment.

Pros: With a little research, it's usually easy to determine why the customer cancelled. The situation that caused the cancellation may have changed within your organization or the customer's.

Cons: Sometimes working this resource is like a walk in a cemetery: no matter how attractive the grounds or artistic the markers, the people are still dead. Some cancelled customers are just dead.

Professional organizations: Many service salespeople are members of organizations that relate directly or indirectly to their markets. Organizations like BOMA (Building Owners and Managers Association), ASHRAE (Association of Heating, Refrigeration and Air Conditioning Engineers), and NFPA (National Fire Protection Association) can be good sources of information and contacts. For some market segments, involvement with the local chamber of commerce may present solid opportunities. One drawback: these types of organizations can be expensive to join and can become time bandits. Do your research before joining. Make sure the membership actually includes people who may be interested in purchasing your services.

Customer referrals: There's nothing better than a satisfied customer giving you the name of a peer at another facility. These are great leads, but unfortunately they're few and far between unless you consistently ask people. If you receive one of these leads, run to a phone and schedule an appointment!

I've purposely saved the best and worst lead sources for last.

The WORST

Cold calling: Scheduled or unscheduled cold calling is the least productive way to prospect. If you're in an industry in which success depends on cold calling, good luck. I've heard tales of people who thrive on cold calling and have consistently overachieved but I consider them folklore. Why would anyone resort to cold calling if they weren't forced to do it? It's unpredictable and, on occasion, humiliating.

However, there are cold calls that make sense. Situations occur when an unscheduled call or visit is appropriate. You may have a hole in your schedule and be conveniently located near a facility or individual that may present an opportunity. You may be visiting a company and uncover a key decision maker or sponsor who is accessible. A news item may motivate a phone call. Although these situations are considered cold calls, in reality they are just a little on the chilly side. If it feels right, go for it. If your prospecting strategy is based solely on cold calling, I wish you the best.

The BEST

Operations staff: Leads from people in your company who actually perform service or are in direct contact with customers are the closest thing to money in the bank. Technicians, dispatchers, administrative people, and service managers are the best sources of prequalified leads. Normally these individuals have high levels of credibility with customers, ranging from respect to devout worship. A service sales representative's career can be impacted significantly by these resources. I speak from experience.

Ponzi Prospecting

In 1919 a man by the name of Charles Ponzi opened an office in the financial section of Boston. Ponzi called his firm the Securities Exchange Company. His prospecting strategy encompassed mailing out hundreds of prospectuses to people who were deemed to have funds available for investment. His offering was compelling: a 50 percent return on investment in forty-five days and 100 percent in ninety days. Not surprisingly, within a short time, he was receiving $500,000 a day and paying out $200,000 a day. Today these figures are large; in 1919 dollars, they were extraordinary.

Thousands of people descended on his office to invest. Historical records show he employed sixteen clerks just to sort and count the money. Trash cans and closets were stuffed with currency. Like most pyramid schemes, when the inflow of cash slowed down, the pyramid collapsed. Ponzi was arrested and, not unlike the more recent situation with Bernard Madoff, the investors blamed it on the government. After serving time in federal prison, Ponzi jumped bail and was caught running pyramid schemes in three states. While Ponzi's scheme is far from the perfect business model, it sure is a great prospecting strategy.

My Honeywell branch office was typical of many found in technical product sales. The territory covered about half the state of New Jersey. The branch housed various management, sales, technical and administrative support people. It had a small service parts warehouse stocked with a minimal amount of standard equipment to support our fifteen technicians. Most only stopped by once a week to pick up materials. Approximately half were union employees.

Most months we had branch meetings with the majority of technicians in attendance. We had a sales force of five, and a branch manager and a sales manager with successful track records.

The circumstances that led to my hire as a service sales representative were typical of most of my peers. I was in my early twenties, had some work experience, and wanted to find something better, and my car was in need of major repairs. My qualifications for the position were suspect, but somehow I aced an aptitude test that guys with the desired engineering degrees had tanked. I clearly remember being mocked before the test by guys flaunting their engineering degrees from cake-eater private schools. I was a lowly accounting major from the local state U.

Ironically I was the only person in a group of twenty or so who passed the test. Go figure. Maybe it was my score, my interview, or my previous experience working for a hat company. Maybe that impressed somebody. Regardless I found myself taking the first step in a career that would become my calling. If not for the red Volare that was part of the job offer, I probably wouldn't have taken the position. Imagine deciding the merits of a job opportunity based on the company car provided. Oh to be young and stupid. Those were the days.

Once hired, I was off to the Midwest for a three-week training session where I was schooled on the technical and sales aspects of the job. I was part of a group of fifteen guys who all had technical backgrounds; I was the exception. Most had solid sales experience under their belts as well. It was clear to me, and everyone else, I was in over my head.

The technical training seemed simple enough, but I didn't find myself stimulated by the conversations like my classmates. The sales training was adequate at best. For some reason it was all focused on doing well on a videotaped role play at the end of the course. There was a resident belief that future success or failure would be determined by one's ability to sell service to the instructor, in front of a video camera hidden behind a mirror, in a tiny room that felt like a sauna at a bad health club.

The night before the role play will always stay with me. Because of it I will forever hold some shred of sympathy for people on death row. I didn't sleep and I felt like I was living a nightmare due to a severe case of hives brought on by the stress of the situation. My fears were not unfounded; when it came time for the role play I did a pitiful job that exceeded my worst expectations. I recall sweating profusely, trembling, babbling, and surviving what I now know was an anxiety attack.

Even though future failure was clearly indicated, I graduated. The bus ride to the airport was a running joke at my expense.

Little did I know that someday most of those guys would be kissing up to me to gain promotions. More important, I would find myself empowered to banish video role playing from the training curriculum in my company (I quickly located my tape and destroyed it) and any company I was ever associated with in the future.

Upon returning to my branch, I was presented with my first quota. I wasn't a technical wiz, and I had questionable sales skills, but as an accounting major, I knew I was screwed. There wasn't any possibility I could succeed or even remotely overachieve. The time I would need to attain my quota exceeded the available hours in a year, including weekends and holidays. I had to come up with a plan.

I felt confident my sales skills were solid, regardless of what the film critics were saying. I also felt my territory held promise and my branch offered a solid support base. My problem was time. Based on the number of proposals I would need to generate, the typical size of an average sale, and the close rates traditionally found in my assigned market, I was already two months behind plan!

Just like Ponzi had, I saw my opportunity for fame and fortune with my own version of the pyramid scheme. I calculated I could find two or three prospects a week if I followed the strategy I'd been taught. Identifying those prospects would probably consume more than half my sales time. I would have to work the phones, do mailings, and even do some dreaded cold calling. If I were aggressive and lucky, I might come into contact with a dozen potential prospects in a week.

On the other hand my company had fifteen technicians who averaged three service calls a day, a dispatcher who spoke with dozens of customers daily, and a technical management team that always seemed to be salivating over blueprints. It looked something like this:

Joe	1 x 2 prospects/day x 5 days = **10** prospects visits/week
Technicians	15 x 3 visits/day x 5 days = **225** customer visits/ week
Dispatcher	50 customers/day x 5 days = **250** customer contacts/week
SCORE	HOME: **475** VISITOR: **10**

Of course the majority of clients the technicians and dispatcher dealt with were already customers. On the other hand, many of these customers had problems that needed to be addressed or levels of service that were less than ideal. Having made more than a few visits to Atlantic City's new casinos, I knew the house always wins. I was going to place my bet on the house—in this case my branch and its skilled technicians.

Immediately I set my plan into action. Within a few short weeks, I had connected with every technician and bowed at the feet of my dispatcher daily. I knew the names of their children, significant others, pets, and birthdays. I always had the time and patience to listen to their stories and their problems at work or home. I had their lunch routines down and was practiced in the wizardry, long before J.K. Rowling made the skill fashionable, of making their favorite donuts appear. I made it a priority to meet them on jobsites with the repair parts they needed in hand.

I also made sure they knew what type of opportunities I was looking for and my commitment to a quick follow-up. Not only was I building a great affinity with this group, but I was also getting to know some great people. I could never understand how other service salespeople overlooked this resource. These individuals help people for a living. All they require in return is respect and some well-deserved gratitude. I had plenty of both to give.

Almost immediately leads started coming in. It began when a couple of technicians suggested I visit their accounts, which I did immediately. I soon provided them updates on what had taken place and my plan of action. Regardless of the outcome they were getting treated to lunch and a sincere thank you for their efforts.

Within weeks it developed into the majority of our staff leaving leads on my desk. Some included complete surveys, many already presold. I was only spending a couple of hours a week actually prospecting, and those were spent on the largest accounts in my territory. I had the luxury of time, which allowed me to develop key accounts without depending on them for immediate sales.

Soon I was spending most of my sales time preparing proposals and presenting them to customers. The volume grew so great it required spending most Saturdays at the office, processing orders and catching up on paperwork. My pyramid scheme was working.

I did everything possible to make sure I kept the deposits coming. I published my own newsletter highlighting leads submitted by the technicians, regardless if they materialized in sales. I conducted my own sales contests to reward them. My tactics created some jealousy and resentment from the other salespeople, but I made my annual quota in six months. Most important, I developed admiration for the people who had the skills and desire to show up every day at our customers' sites and take care of their problems.

Other salespeople I worked with had the same opportunity to develop this important relationship but chose to do otherwise. I was amazed by how many times I would hear my peers making excuses for why they hadn't yet followed up on leads technicians had given them. Rarely did these sales professionals take the time to visit a jobsite or buy a lunch. But they would proudly accept congratulations at branch sales meetings, often without acknowledging the technicians responsible for initiating the sales. Not surprisingly some went on to successful careers in product sales.

Pyramid schemes fail when receipts can't keep up with payouts. In my case receipts grew as our branch added technicians to support our growing business. Over time we grew from fifteen to twenty to twenty-five technicians. The problem I couldn't control was my sales manager's desire to hire more salespeople. Eventually my territory shrank and my quota grew. I wasn't going to wait around too long and see my pyramid collapse. I beat it out of town ahead of the authorities and accepted a marketing position at headquarters.

Summary

Service sales prospecting requires a significant amount of time and commitment. It also requires some creativity. I feel safe in saying people who achieve consistent service sales success implement the time-proven prospecting strategies their companies recommend. I also feel safe in saying people who overachieve in service sales augment traditional methods with their own schemes for success.

Overachieving requires stepping back and examining what you're doing. You need to look beyond the norms of your company. Service salespeople must be creative in developing methods that complement their particular social styles, skills, and goals. What is the average amount of time you spend arranging, traveling to, and participating in one sales call? Two hours? Three hours? More? Why would you ever want to waste your time with someone who is less than a perfect prospect?

Chapter 5

QUALIFYING
THE HOLY GRAIL

The Holy Grail has been a figure in literature, religion, and, more recently, books and movies. The first known reference is said to have been made in the twelfth century in Robert de Boron's *Joseph d'Arimathie*. It is believed to possess miraculous powers. Is it a plate, a cup, a dish? Does it even exist?

Whatever the reality, it symbolizes something with special powers. Who can resist the thought that somewhere there is something that, if recovered, will address some of life's great mysteries? Ever notice when the Holy Grail is mentioned in a book or movie the characters take it very seriously and immediately accept the fact that it exists and any opportunity to recover it is worth life or limb? Personally I like Monty Python's humorous spin on it.

Why the Holy Grail reference? First I believe the qualifying step in the sales cycle is where the magic happens. If done correctly it has the miraculous power to create superstar service salespeople. It can transform a mediocre prospect into a "where do I sign" customer. It can expose a fraudulent prospect and identify the path to the kingmaker. Second I want you to read this chapter as if you just found a long-lost document in your great-grandmother's trunk that will lead you to the greatest discovery of your career. Visualize a Nicholas Cage movie promo.

In all seriousness I believe the qualification step in the sales cycle is the most important by far. It dictates and impacts everything else in the sales cycle. Based on my analysis of thousands of sold, lost, or abandoned proposals, the information uncovered during the qualification stage is the primary reason for success or failure over eighty percent of the time.

I've never understood why qualifying doesn't get more attention and focus. There are countless books and articles about closing sales. Closing is sexy. Everyone loves people who can close the deal. Qualifying, on the other hand, lacks sex appeal. The term isn't always understood when discussing sales. It also doesn't lend itself well to a simple formula...or does it? I will prove otherwise later in this chapter.

Have you ever heard anyone brag about being the best salesperson on the planet because she's an awesome qualifier? I doubt it. It's the closers that get the glory. In reality closing an order is only possible when a prospective customer has been properly qualified. Great closers are made because they're great qualifiers, even if they don't know it.

Mariano Rivera may be the best closer in the history of baseball. His ability to get three outs in the ninth inning is remarkable. But as any baseball fan knows, you can't record a save unless you have the opportunity. That means your team put you in the position during the previous eight innings to come in and close the game out. A star closer in sales has to pitch the whole game.

Qualifying is an interesting term. As I've mentioned it's not in everyone's sales lexicon. I can often tell by people's expressions they're not quite sure what I'm speaking about. I've become accustomed to breaking it down to an example that everyone understands. It's the step in the sales process where you determine if the prospect is worthy of more of your time and commitment to seeking his business. Once again I find it interesting that it's the most important step in the sales cycle and the only one not clearly labeled in the sales profession. If you look in a dictionary, *qualify* is described in various ways, including:

- To make less general and more restrictive
- To certify or license, as in qualified to practice law
- To exhibit needed fitness, skill, or ability for some end

I think the second bullet is the closest to how I interpret the term. We qualify prospects to determine if they meet the necessary criteria to become potential customers. In reality the salesperson is certifying, based on established criteria, the prospect is or is not a qualified prospect. Once that standard is met, it's time to move to the next step in the sales cycle. If that standard is not met, moving forward typically results in failure.

Attempting to sell an unqualified prospect is a waste of everyone's time. So why do salespeople do it every day? There are many reasons, but I think the primary issue is not understanding what is required to qualify a prospect. Many companies and sales representatives don't spend the time to develop their own criteria for determining if a prospect is qualified. I'm not 100 percent certain how I came to my own conclusions on the information needed. I do know once I established my list it became part of every sales organization I managed. I continue to train every class I teach in what information is absolutely necessary to gather during the qualifying sales call.

To aid in the process, I introduce an acronym, WFAN, that can be used on every call. The simple formula also helps when discussing and analyzing sales activity at all levels. It introduces discipline into the sales process. The ultimate goal is to develop a qualification-centric sales strategy. That means providing proposals only to qualified prospects. Gone are the days of generating a quote for anyone we think we could remotely sell. Platitudes should no longer be issued to those who have bloated quote logs. Success is measured by generating sales, not quotes.

There are those who contend one begets the other. True statement, but it's a generalization that needs closer examination. Some companies operate like quote mills. The goal is simple: quote, quote, and quote some more. Quotes are produced and hung like wallpaper. Proposal backlogs resemble a list of New Year's resolutions that once again will not be fulfilled. I'm certain there is a productive service-business model somewhere that utilizes the "quote first and qualify later" strategy effectively, but I've never seen it.

I have always been candid in telling my service sales representatives what they were paid to do. The old school would say sell, sell, sell. My mantra is "qualify, qualify, qualify." The cornerstone of my training classes is always the qualifying section. I spend, by far, the most time covering this subject.

In my opinion selling is both an art and a science. It's very difficult to teach art to those who are not so inclined, like me. In sales the artistic side comes into play in the form of interpersonal communications, abstract thinking, creativity, and other areas that are not easy to formulize. You either have it or you don't.

In some cases training may be helpful in maximizing a person's skill set, but dramatic changes in behavior are rare. I also believe science can be applied to service sales. In this case *science* refers to the ability to apply theories and formulas to areas in the sales process. The step that needs the most attention, requires both sales skill sets, and lacks the most structure is qualifying.

Challenges

Who to Contact

The first person you meet or speak with when qualifying a new account has ramifications in both time and effort. Wasting time calling on the wrong person can not only cost you valuable sales time but it can also have a negative impact on developing the account. Call on the wrong person and he may discourage you from proceeding or even torpedo your effort to meet the right person.

It's also not unusual to hear misleading information regarding the current situation, which may reduce your desire to proceed. On the other hand, calling on the right person, even at the wrong level, may reveal important information that can be utilized moving forward. Regardless, identifying and speaking with the right person should be the goal.

That begs the question, who is the right person? Typically there are three levels of potential contacts in most service sales situations. Additionally there may be multiple people at each level.

Sponsor—I consider anyone who can influence a sale but not make a purchasing decision a sponsor. The level of influence at the sponsor level is broad. Some sponsors have the ability to guide a proposal to the right person, all but putting a pen in her hand to sign it. There are others who have little or no influence on the situation but talk a good game. These individuals are particularly dangerous as they may play the "don't go around me" card. A service salesperson who is solely dependent on a sponsor to get a proposal approved has put his fate in someone else's hands—obviously not a place your want to be.

Sponsors come in all shapes and sizes. Some will be forthcoming with key information while others may be playing a game at your expense. They can help or they can hinder. For instance if your service offering jeopardizes the sponsor's position or his staff's, you may find yourself in a no-win situation. If your service solution needs to be justified based on ROI that includes staff reductions, it's imperative that you enter the account at an executive level. People with profit and lose responsibility will be more responsive to spending reductions even if they require staff reductions. Sponsors can also protect a preferred vendor or use you to support their current situations by requesting overloaded service agreements that will be used as cost hammers to justify their value to their superiors.

Unfortunately the service sales profession gets caught in the sponsor trap all too often. This is most typified when leads come from company technicians who have relationships with operational people at a site. "I told Joey, their maintenance guy, you'll be calling him tomorrow"—that's a typical scenario that all too often leads service salespeople to the wrong points of contact. I'm sure Joey is a great guy with the best intentions, but is he the right person needed to qualify this account?

It's very common that the person who purchased the equipment or is operating it is not the right person to contact when selling service. Many people choose that path because their contact information is usually available, making the research required simple. For some products or systems, the person who was involved in purchasing the equipment may also be the right contact with whom to pursue a service relationship. For many others the service decision is made somewhere else, maybe at a distant location.

For example in the life-safety service market, most systems are sold through subcontractors, not to the building owners or operators. Calling on the engineering firm or contractor who installed the equipment is a waste of time. The service salesperson needs to identify the person responsible for operating the facility. Trying to sell service through an intermediary sponsor is risky business. All too often it looks, sounds, and feels right, but in most cases it's otherwise.

Authorizing party—In many organizations the person who authorizes the service purchase is the key individual. Often this person may have the authority to process the order but may be far removed from the situation. Most often this is the case when a support function like purchasing, legal, or remote management is involved. These people are usually part of the purchasing process due to company policy put in place to ensure established guidelines and procedures are met.

To people in service sales, they are the dark side. They put distance and a barrier between us and our client. They weren't present for our perfect sales call, at the table for the pricey lunch we paid for, or part of our discussion of client needs. Most frustrating is our inability to communicate our value proposition, as their focus is typically cost or terms and conditions.

In many cases our client contacts have the power to get what they want. Many will even resort to intimidating their own support groups. Unfortunately there are many others who just roll over and cower to the demands of other people and departments within their companies. It's a very helpless feeling; we've all experienced it.

Some service salespeople do great jobs of getting in front of these bureaucrats while others just cast their fate to the wind. This is a classic situation of failure in the qualifying process. If the prospect were qualified correctly, the role of all involved is known upfront. This allows the salesperson to do what's necessary to guide the proposal through the process. If this information is not known ahead of time, the service salesperson is usually rewarded with a dose of humble pie and, typically, a lost sale.

Decision makers—A prospect should never be considered qualified unless the decision makers are identified and their scope of responsibly is known. This is not a gray area. This is a must-know, no-excuse, punishable-by-death event if there is any lack of clarity regarding who will make the final decision to purchase the service agreement.

It is inexcusable to propose a service agreement to anyone who is not the decision maker. It's also the most common reason service agreements are not sold and service salespeople have poor close rates. Often service salespeople are too trusting: "No problem. Joey said he'll get the proposal approved. They always accept his recommendations." Not to exaggerate, but I think I've heard this statement, with only the name changing, a thousand times.

I've also been the victim of this game many times. The outcome is usually the same: I keep following up with Joey, time passes, and then I'm forced to come to the realization the order is not coming. That requires going back to the account, circumventing Joey, getting an audience with the actual decision maker, and rekindling the whole deal. Even when it's successful, many hours have been wasted, costing me valuable sales time that could be spent with other prospects.

Truth or Dare?

I believe all people are inherently good. People are honest, fair, and forthcoming. Surprisingly I still believe this after a career in sales. Most salespeople assume the information they receive from a prospect is factual. There should be no reason to think otherwise. Why would a prospect supply misinformation to a salesperson? If you're not grinning after reading that statement, you're not an experienced salesperson—or you're a really bad one.

As previously mentioned most people don't like being sold. Many prospective clients have their guards up whenever they encounter a salesperson. Will some contacts only tell you the good stuff, overlooking important information that may limit your opportunity? Yes, deception is inherent in most sales situations. Will some tell you their current providers are excellent and the only way they would switch is if you are cheaper, even if they hold their current suppliers in contempt? Yes, this is an all too common occurrence. Is it possible the prospect will tell you he is the decision maker when he's not? For sure!

I find it interesting that upstanding people find it perfectly acceptable to bend the truth in a buying-selling situation. I think it's one of life's most common double standards.

So how do we verify what we're hearing is reality? Usually it comes down to the duck test: if it walks like a duck, swims like a duck, and quacks like a duck, it must be a duck. Reality is usually found in the situation. The product or system we're pursuing service on has operating parameters based on functionality and usage. The older it gets, the more likely it is to fail. The more it's used, the greater likelihood it needs service. The lack of onsite skills for repair or programming makes response time by trained technicians critical. Lack of onsite inventory makes parts availability a factor. Unfortunately information is often left to interpretation. The information potential customers give to service salespeople almost always contains a little bit of misinformation.

This is another good spot to plug the science aspect of sales. Let's call it CSI: Service Sales. Walk into an aging building with a busy lobby and outdated elevators and ask your contact if there have been any problems. The response may be "no." Ask any occupant in the building if the elevators are ever out of order and you'll probably receive more factual information. Ask a prospect if he ever has any problems with the fire alarm system and you may hear "never" or "rarely." Ask a person standing at a copy machine if she ever hears alarms going off and once again facts will surface. Ask a prospect if she will be making the decision regarding the services you provide and she may tell you "yes." Later in the call ask if her name should appear in the approval space on the agreement and you may hear otherwise.

All of the above examples are common occurrences. Rarely—as in never—will your prospective client exclaim, "Our system is a total mess. We're desperate for someone to repair it at any cost. Give me a proposal today and I'll sign it on the spot and give you a check."

Obviously, accusing a prospective customer of lying is not the best of strategies. It takes a bit of savvy to get the right information. My tactic has always been to provide a gentle nudge back to reality. I make an effort to enlighten the prospect to the norms regarding his system. I congratulate him on how fortunate he has been not to have experienced problems most others have. At the same time I inform him he should be prepared, as storm clouds are on the horizon. It takes skill and sensitivity to convey this information in a positive way that doesn't question the client's integrity but enlightens him about the potential risks of forgoing necessary maintenance or service on his equipment or system.

In the Moment

You scheduled the appointment three weeks ago. The account has the potential to make or break your quota for the quarter. Mr. Dee Cisionmaker is looking forward to the meeting. He has mentioned he just lost his top technical staff member and will not be replacing him.

You get up at 5:00 a.m. to ensure you can cover the ninety-mile drive and arrive with time to spare. Your daughter just got accepted into Princeton, your husband finally agreed to take that trip to Paris, and your boss just approved your 11 percent raise. You're patiently waiting in your client's outer office, reflecting on how great you feel having just dropped fifteen pounds. All is right with the world.

Mr. Dee Cisionmaker's assistant guides you to his office and asks you to be seated. Dee enters, slides into his chair, and slams down a file, cursing under his breath as he looks at you with the face of doom. You ask him if it's a bad time for the meeting and offer to reschedule.

He replies, "You're here. I'm here. Let's just get it over with."

All is no longer right with the world, but you proceed, immediately aware what you are saying is not registering with your prospect. The call ends abruptly, your request to submit a proposal is graciously accepted, you're screwed, and you know it. You head out, but before exiting you have a quick chat with the assistant. You hope she can shed some light on what has just transpired.

The time you spend building this rapport pays off. She tells you: "Mr. Dee Cisionmaker noticed upon arriving this morning that his prized, eighty-eight Mercedes had been keyed last night. There was an e-mail this morning that said he needs to have his budget forecast ready for a meeting at one o'clock today rather than on Monday, and he needs to cut twenty percent off the bottom line. He also received a call from the VP of human resources informing him he is the subject of a sexual harassment claim filed by an unidentified staff member." The assistant believes those items may have irritated him a bit but feels news that his pay has been garnished for back alimony has ticked him off the most.

Obviously the above scenario is a huge embellishment, but there is a sales lesson lurking inside. Every day salespeople meet with prospects and customers who have real lives. We know them as manager of this, director of that, and most commonly as potential commission checks. We have no idea what's going on in their lives. We assume they are immune to forces both inside and outside of their offices. They have no problems beyond maintaining the equipment we've come to talk about.

Those of us with an overblown perception of self-importance actually think everyone wants to see us and even likes us. I'm sorry to break it to you, but you do grate on some people, and they would rather have a colonoscopy than meet with you.

Regardless of the situation, we need be aware that our clients are real people with real issues. An experienced service salesperson usually picks up the signals early on. The difficult decision is whether to proceed with the meeting or ask for a time-out. My experience tells me the worst thing to do is ignore the problem and continue on. Would you like to listen to a salesperson when you just found out your child was suspended for the third time or your doctor called and said he'd like to take another X-ray?

I see three options:

- Ask for permission to proceed. In almost all cases, the client will wave off his concerns and tell you to continue with the call. Based on the time you've already invested and your upcoming busy month, you continue. Chances for success are poor.

- Be a counselor. Drop your script and see if you can open up a discussion focused on your client's issues in hope that dialogue, or just listening, will settle her down. This can be a very effective strategy if done correctly. Many people welcome the opportunity to blow off some steam. We've all heard things in sales calls that rival what we could hear from a bar mate at 2:00 a.m.

At the same time there are people who want their personal issues kept private. Any attempt to enter their inner sanctums will be met with contempt. People's lives are complicated, and emotions can run high. I think offering your client the opportunity to express herself is a good way to build rapport, but you need to be confident that you can handle it.

- Suggest rescheduling. There's nothing more frustrating than having to reschedule a call when you're already onsite. It requires discipline to act professional and not let your emotions get the best of you. Imagine yourself in the shoes of the salesperson in the example: a half day wasted, a potential sale that may be postponed at least a month, and an uncomfortable discussion with a sales manager who wants to know how the call went. Rationalizing the situation is easy with a clear head. Will my chances for making a sale be better or worse if I reschedule the call? Will my ability to discuss my company's value proposition and explore the client's operational issues be more effective with a focused client?

In most cases taking the high road and strongly suggesting another meeting is the best tactic. Typically your sensitivity to the situation will be appreciated, and your relationship will start off on a positive note. With that said, if you just spent a day traveling to the appointment and have $1,200 in expenses, either of the first two options may be a better alternative.

Reboot or Delete

There's a point in every qualifying call when you know if you've got a great opportunity or something less. You've asked all of the important questions and received answers that are credible. They may not be what you were hoping for, but they are what they are. You tried every sales angle you have in your bag of tricks, but nothing is working. Reality starts to set in and you know you're in trouble.

The pit in your stomach grows as you see another opportunity die and another incentive check shrink. Once again self-doubt regarding your sales skills sets in. Many—far too many—service salespeople get desperate and discard professional selling skills and switch to survival mode. They promise discounts, bad-mouth competitors, present a case of Armageddon if the prospect's equipment fails, or, even worse, bellow, "I'll send you a proposal."

What many can't do is just come to grips with the fact that not every prospect becomes a qualified prospect. If they did, anyone could become an overachieving service salesperson.

Of all the life preservers available in a Titanic sales call, the one that most upsets me is the worthless proposal. Admit it: you've sent a proposal to a prospect that had little or no chance of purchasing your services. We all have. Some feel it's our patriotic duty to do what we think we're paid to do—quote and sell. We've all been informed, on many occasions, no quotes means no sales. Who hasn't been called to task when their quote backlog is less than expected?

We've all fallen victim to the dated sales myth that claims quoting everything and everyone is the right thing to do. There are also psychological factors that make us go through this worthless exercise. For many it's the need to feel like something was accomplished. Unless your sales process requires only minutes to generate a quote and you're absolutely sure you've talked to the right person, it's wrong. If you're selling service on equipment or systems that require a site survey, cumbersome data input, or gaining approvals, it should be avoided.

Try computing the time it takes to put together and generate a solid proposal for one of your clients. This doesn't mean just the time sitting at a computer doing the task, but also the time set aside to compile the information, update your database, compose a cover e-mail or letter, present or forward the proposal, enter it into your backlog, discuss it with your manager, follow up on the proposal a couple of times, and, the hardest to compute, the number of times you thought about it and rationalized you may still get the order.

I would rather have good information about a potential client for future use than have one of my proposals reside with the wrong person, with the wrong offering and price in their files. I not only have exposed my lack of skills and poor judgment in submitting a proposal to an unqualified prospect, but it may also be used against me in the future. All too often old proposals are used as discussion points when making qualifying calls— once again a good reason to research a client before making the first call.

Do you reboot the prospect and look for another angle or person in the organization who may resurrect the situation? If you can identify one, then rebooting may be the way to go. If not it's time to leave your card, thank the prospect for his time, and revisit the account sometime in the near future. Unqualified prospects in service sales are like zombies. They hang around until someone cuts their heads off. Once that's done a hero surfaces and they need you to help bring sanity to their crazy world. Don't ever write off any account. People change, situations change, and quite often new strategies come into play as you gain experience.

Qualifying Steps
- Preparation

    The most important ingredient to a successful first/qualifying call is done before the meeting is even scheduled. The fundamental question is who to contact. Often this information can be obtained through an internal effort, such as researching customer data in company records. Contact information can also come in the form of a lead from a technician, a salesperson, or someone else in your organization.

    Regardless of where the contact information originates, it needs to be qualified further. This is a particularly important step as on many occasions the person identified is not the best option. Once again the goal is to meet with the person who is responsible for making the service purchasing decision, not a sponsor.

    Like many sales positions service sales is a top-down sales strategy. This point always generates debate as everyone has tales of success that came from starting with personnel using the equipment and working up the decision-making ladder. Working upstream maybe required for a salmon, but not a service sales representative. Entering an account at a low level or mid-level should be the exception, not a rule.

On the other hand, contacting someone at a higher level can result in a referral to someone lower in the organization. This is usually a good scenario, as you meet the support staff member as directed by Mr. Big. Alternatively a service salesperson can do a great sales job at the lower level, but then the proposal fails when management shoots down the lower level sponsor. This is a helpless situation that not only costs a sale but can also distance the service salesperson from her sponsor after the sponsor has been rejected by his superiors.

Once the correct contact point is determined, a solid grounding on any previous relationship with the account is needed. Often there is past history with both the prospective client and the business. This requires some research and seeking out people who may have had previous interactions with the account. Past experiences can shed some light on potential barriers as well as opportunities.

This research phase is a good time to uncover who is currently servicing the account. If it's a competitor there is normally some local-market insight, based on their reputation, pricing strategy, or account management that you can use to your benefit. There is also the possibility that an in-house staff member may be servicing the equipment. In short you should never approach a prospective client ignorant of any history with your company or the client's current service arrangement.

For many service salespeople, live, in-person sales calls are the norm. This is typically the case when the service revenue potential is large, geographical territory is condensed, or the equipment needs a high level of technician-customer interaction. For others phone and electronic communication are the most economical ways to market service.

However, when it comes to qualifying a potential customer, there is no substitute for a face-to-face sales call. Service is a relationship business. It requires a certain level of trust to purchase a service agreement, and that's difficult to gain when communicating across miles. When you gain insight into the customer's business firsthand, you're in a better position to have an expanded dialogue that will help in the overall qualification process. If a service salesperson can only make one live sales call and the choices are information gathering, qualifying, surveying, or closing, I would choose qualifying every time.

• Appointment

Gaining an appointment is often a challenge. The people we are trying to connect with are usually overburdened and guard their time. One major hurdle is getting by the gatekeepers.

There was a time when the primary gatekeeper was a secretary or assistant. You would make a phone call to the targeted contact, a gatekeeper would answer, and you would have to give her a palatable story before she would grant you access to your prospect. Those were certainly the good old days. That was a time when a good salesperson could turn on the charm and usually get access to the necessary person.

Sometimes the gatekeepers were bulldogs digging in their heels, but at least you had opportunities to offer them biscuits. In almost all cases perseverance was rewarded and appointments would be granted. Today voicemail and e-mail have become the gatekeepers. The "delete" button has turned mild-mannered individuals into empowered control freaks. Spammers complicate our efforts as they constantly assault our potential clients. Fighting spam has created a whole new service business. Ironically advances in this area have wrongfully identified many service sales communications as spam. Service salespeople are pitted against rogues selling Viagra and Facebook introduction requests.

My suggestions, keep your communications short, and provide a sample. If you've ever been in a Costco or a Sam's Club, you've probably seen hair-netted people giving away samples of products; typically a crowd of people patiently await the next batch of baked beans or a tortilla chip in a little, white cup. Sometimes a little box of cereal or bottle of lotion comes in the mail or with your newspaper, assuming you still get one. Are we attracted to samples because they're free or are we afraid we may be missing out on something? I don't normally partake in these activities, but I've watched people push and shove to get a tiny taste of some must-have lentil soup as if it came from the just-discovered fountain of youth.

When you leave a voicemail or communicate by e-mail, you are giving a sample of who you are. The receiving party gets a brief taste of your personality and what they may expect to see or hear upon meeting you. Obviously you need to explain your intention, but just as important, you must entice a person to meet with you.

Voicemails come in all shapes and sizes. Some sound like the person leaving the message is suffering from depression while others sound like digital voices. I receive messages that are painful to listen to as the person rambles on with little forethought of what to say. Maybe the most irritating are the simple name, number, "call me" messages. Sure, like that's going to happen.

- o Voicemail—good

    "Mr. Important, my name is Alexa. I'm a service sales representative with Mammoth Machine. I'd appreciate the opportunity to stop by and introduce myself and the services we offer to help you maintain your system. I look forward to hearing from you."

o Voicemail—bad

"Hi, I'm calling in reference to your Mammoth system AF876-2356 that was purchased by someone there... let me see...last October. My mistake, I mean last September. According to our records your system hasn't been serviced and may be out of warranty. Normally by now we've done preventive maintenance on a system like yours, but according to our records that's not the case. I'm assuming you're the person responsible for the Mammoth system, but if you're not I hope you can lead me to the right person. Our records show you as the contact person. Anyway I'd like to talk to you about a service contract on the system. Our service contracts are great values compared to other companies'. By the way do your know Shelly Conlon? She's my sister in-law and she said she thinks she met you at a party. Anyway if you get a chance give me a buzz. I'm usually on the road, but I'll give you my cell number, my office number, and my e-mail. Give me a call when you get a chance."

o Voicemail—ugly

"Sorry, a bus just passed by. I hope you can hear me. Mr. Important, Alexa over at Mammoth, call me if you'd like to talk about a service contract."

In the first example not only was there clarity in the message, but Alexa came across as non-aggressive and professional. The information was relayed in a style that respected the potential client's time restrictions and at the same time conveyed a positive impression of the salesperson. If the client didn't respond it left the door open for another voicemail without being perceived as annoying or confrontational.

The bad example creates an image of a person who is disconnected, impersonal, and boring. I wouldn't be surprised if the next message left by this individual were deleted once her name was conveyed.

As for the ugly, it sounds absurd, but calls similar to this are made every day when salespeople operate in a multitasking, spontaneous mode. Has texting impacted the way we communicate by phone and e-mail? It's hard to make a case that it hasn't. I'm sure there are people who claim texting has forced us to be more concise with our communication. I'm not one of those people.

E-mail presents a big problem. It's great for forwarding and following up on proposals. It's also an effective method for answering questions or rescheduling appointments. When e-mail is the communication method for introducing yourself or for setting up an appointment, it's often problematic. Will your e-mail be read, deleted, or identified as spam? Do you have the right e-mail address? Has it been forwarded to the wrong person?

These are all good questions with no definitive answers. Experience tells me the most important part of an e-mail is the subject line. It's important for evading spam blockers, and it needs to resonate with the intended reader. The challenge has become more complicated as more people are reading their e-mails on smartphone's and not looking at large screens. Less space requires crisper messaging. Again, no silver bullet here, but keeping the messaging short, relevant, and congenial will aid your effort.

- Call Structure

    Service sales calls come in all shapes and sizes—relaxed, intense, abrupt, hurried, adversarial, friendly, congenial, informative, etc., and all too often a complete waste of time. They are held in offices, cubicles, boardrooms, labs, basements, restaurants, elevators, hallways, classrooms, loading docks, plant floors, hangars, and a myriad of other places. They are conducted with background noise including machinery, moaning patients, vulgar prisoners, phone interruptions, and angry hotel guests. They are set in locations that are too hot, too cold, and lit to make everyone look like recent vampire victims.

A multitude of environments must be dealt with when trying to conduct a professional qualifying call. In some cases an astute service salesperson may request a change in venue such as a company cafeteria or lobby, but for the most part a sales person just has to deal with the cards that are dealt.

One variable that can't be overlooked is time limitation. Almost all clients have a limited amount of time to spend with a salesperson. There are clients who will do everything in their power to get a sales representative out of their sight as fast as possible. On the other hand there are those who can spend hours chatting away on wide-ranging subjects. A realistic goal would be one quality, uninterrupted half hour. Consider anything beyond that a bonus. Assume more than that and you may be ushered out sooner than expected.

Sometimes the client will immediately set the time limit at the beginning of the meeting. Ironically, I find when this is the case the call almost always runs long. If a client doesn't set a time limit I suggest asking for a specific window before starting. If, for instance, a service salesperson asks if a half hour is available and the client apologizes and says he has only fifteen minutes, it may be best to reschedule. Rushing through a qualifying call will not typically produce the information required. It's the responsibility of the service salesperson to manage the time allotted and request additional time or another meeting.

So there you are sitting in a strange place, with someone you've never laid eyes on, with the goal of selling him something. Before a sale is made you have to determine if you are speaking to the correct individual, what specific needs he has, what financial or political barriers may exist, a timeline for the purchase, and other pertinent information. You not only have about half an hour, but you actually only have about five to ten minutes to engage the prospective client in productive conversation. The key word is *productive*.

Every salesperson has their unique personality and style they bring to a meeting. As I mentioned before, I believe selling has aspects of both science and art. From my perspective the artistry comes in the form of relating to people and the ability to communicate seamlessly. It also includes the ability to craft the perfect proposal that maximizes the company's value proposition.

Science comes in the form of understanding the metrics and best practices of the particular service sales position, e.g. close rates, contact level, ROI calculations, plan development, and implementation. I think it's an almost impossible task to teach a person the artistic skills required. When it comes to the science of service sales I'm confident almost everyone can be trained on the tools and skills. No place is this more evident than on the qualifying call. Every service salesperson needs to know what the goal is, what information is needed, and what the best tactics are for gaining that information.

Let's review the scenario. You walk into a strange environment, meet a person who you may have briefly spoken with on the phone, you have about half an hour to complete the call, and in all honesty you have some anxiety. That makes knowing what your first question is each and every time important. It gets the call off to a solid start by gaining useful information, gives you solid insight into the social style of the client (analytical, amiable, driver, expressive), and you get a chance to sit back, listen, and formulate the second question. This question is so powerful it gives insight into the client and the client's world. Let's not underestimate the client's world, which, to a great degree, revolves around his paycheck. So what's the question? I'll get to that shortly.

• Goal

The goal of a qualifying call is to assess if the client is worthy of further attention and time. The options are: deem the prospect qualified, seek out another person within the organization, or walk away. If the person is deemed a qualified prospect, then the next step, before departing, is to review the critical points in the discussion and suggest a plan of action. That plan may include needed access to additional information, a site survey, sending a proposal, presenting a proposal, or another meeting. It's usually the service salesperson's call to make—justifiably, so it's her time and effort that will be required to move to the next step in the service sales cycle.

Qualifying Made Easy

Determining if the prospect is qualified requires answers to specific information. The key word here is *specific*. A salesperson can leave a call with a pad full of information, installation schematics, and a myriad of information, but it may not be what is needed to pursue a sale. Clients may be forthcoming and surrender every detail regarding the equipment and the need for service but still be unqualified.

I've seen lengthy lists of questions companies recommend their salespeople ask. Dozens of example questions are listed, all with merit: Are you the decision maker? How old is the system? How much did you spend on service calls last year? If you could design your own service agreement what would it include? All good questions, but too often they generate vague and redundant answers. For a new-hire service salesperson, the question choices are often overwhelming.

Based on my experiences and those of my clients, it's clear the majority of lost orders for new and experienced service salespeople are due to poor qualifying. In most cases prospects were never qualified and should not have received proposals. Unqualified prospects do not buy; they waste your time.

My challenge was to simplify the question set. This was where science came into play. From my perspective, to be deemed a qualified prospect, four key criteria must be met. Not three, not six, but four. The process starts by asking:

- **The Question**

I pose a question to every class I train. I've been asking it for years. "What's the first question you ask after you greet the client?"

My question usually generates the same responses:

"How's it going?"

"How can I help you?"

"Is that your son/daughter/dog in that picture behind you?"

"Did you catch that swordfish?"

These are typical replies and I assert they are all wastes of time. Rarely do I hear what I'm looking for.

I explain how everyone has probably asked The Question a thousand times. It may not be asked first or on every call, but typically it's asked sooner or later. That usually generates confused looks, but on occasion someone confidently yells out the answer: *How's business?* It may need to be adapted to a particular situation. Common variations include:

"How's your occupancy rate?"

"How are sales compared to last year?"

"How have things gone since the merger?"

These are questions that register with the client. They are in his or her domain. Sometimes the answer will be short, lacking significant information. Such a response gives you a signal that your client may not be very expressive or may be preoccupied. On many occasions the client will share too much information, even conveying opinions about her staff and superiors. The Question is more than the usual small talk that many people overindulge in. It's direct without being intrusive. It's revealing without the sense of being an inquisition.

And, not to be overlooked, it demonstrates your concern for the individual and not just the business you are seeking to gain. It's a people-to-people question, not a salesperson-to-client question. In this case it's a win-win, as you learn about your client and their company you may gather information that addresses one or more of the big four qualifying criteria.

- **WFAN**

The big four—**w**illingness, **f**unding, **a**uthority, and **n**eed—are the main focus of the qualifying call. Three out of four will not do. Based on statistics generated from more than 100,000 service-agreement proposals and more than one hundred companies, lacking the necessary information in any one of these areas will reduce the probability of closing by 50 percent; any two increases that number to, 75 percent.

In no particular order or priority, each of these criteria must be resolved during the call. The information can be gathered from question responses, information like titles, equipment condition, or previous history with the client. When accurate and verifiable information is not forthcoming, assumptions have to be made. Regardless, positive responses to all four—W, F, A, and N—are required to deem a prospect qualified. Let's look at the requirements in more depth.

- **Willingness**

Every salesperson has faced immovable, dig-their-feet-in, not-buying-what-you're-selling, unwilling prospects. They test our patience, grate on our nerves, and leave us questioning our abilities. We made our best efforts, used all of our "works every time" tactics, and may have defaulted to the strategy of last resort: selling price. The client appears to have listened, even asked questions, but in the end it was clear—no service sale for you today. Next!

You leave frustrated, confused and disappointed. Hopefully you didn't promise to send a proposal and add insult to your already damaged ego. Based on the interview, you're sure they're the decision makers and have no funding issues, and the need for service is apparent. So why are they unwilling to purchase your service? What's up with that?

There's no simple answer when trying to analyze the rationales of unwilling prospects. Even in cases when you are clearly told why they will not purchase your service, beware. Often the reasons provided are attempts to explain irrational things in rational ways. For example, I recall an unwilling prospect that made it quite clear he would not buy a service agreement from my company because our service was poor. This came as a surprise as he had called, and continued to call, for service on his system. Both our dispatcher and the technician who serviced the account had nothing but positive comments about the client. He never had any complaints.

Added to the situation was the fact I had made the appointment due to a technician's lead. The technician told me the client wanted to see a sales person. Rather than confront the prospect I decided to ask my technician for help. The next time he went to the site he asked the client if he thought our service was poor. The answer, which I would hear a few additional times over the years from others, was: "I always tell salespeople what they're selling isn't good. If I tell them they're good they'll charge me more. I also know if I buy a service contract your company won't respond as fast. You'll have me locked in and will take advantage of me. I'm happy with the arrangement I have."

Needless to say this type of response is frustrating. No matter what you say or do, the individual has a predetermined bias that isn't easy to change. Some comments from unwilling prospects:

- "I don't believe in service contracts."
- "Why do I need a contract when I can just call you?"
- "I only buy service from manufacturers."
- "I never buy service from manufacturers, it's too expensive."
- "We're selling the building."
- "I only deal with local companies."
- "Our company is being acquired so we're not entering into any new contracts."
- "I know your branch manager. He's a thief/liar/Socialist/ etc."
- "My relative used to work for your company and you fired him. I'll never do business with you!"
- "I like my current service company. Their salesperson attends my church."

Any service salesperson could add to this list with ease. But it's certainly possible to turn an unwilling prospect into a qualified prospect. That's what sales is all about. Listen, analyze, and convey information that may change a person's position. If that happens, then obviously he is no longer unwilling. I'm talking about the person who, after all sales tactics have been exhausted, remains unwilling. Not having "W" makes him an unqualified prospect. Don't tell yourself otherwise. Game over for now, move on, and check back at a later date.

• Funding

There was a time when I used the word *budget* instead of *funding*. They may seem to convey the same message, but that is not the case. A budget is a predetermined amount of money typically set annually. It is a financial goal and constraint. Anyone who has managed a budget knows the endgame is to spend less than you're allotted. That bodes well for the individual by giving a positive impression to superiors.

Once approved a budget is available for spending. In reality that isn't always the scenario. Many individuals hold back spending until late in the year in case some unforeseen event occurs. Others will spend early in the cycle, before anticipated cuts are made. It's also not uncommon, especially in a down economy, for budgets to be reduced during the year. One ironic exception is government agencies that know if they don't spend their whole budgets they may be reduced the following year.

Funding is a broader term. Funding for services may be drawn from multiple accounts in most businesses. There is usually more flexibility when discussing funding rather than budgets. Budgets typically fall into operating and capital with many subareas. Funding includes those areas but may also be drawn from expense accounts used for day-to-day operations in many financial structures.

There's another important difference between the two words. A budget is usually controlled by an individual who has final approval. Asking a person if she has a budget for a service agreement is actually two questions in one. First, has money been set aside for the purchase of service agreements? Second, is it your budget? The answers could be any combination of "yes" and "no." If the answer is "no" to the first question, you face a barrier. If the answer is "no" to the second question, you may have broached an issue that questioned your client's stature in her company. Good information, but not the best method for attaining it.

Is funding available for service? Stating the question in this format opens up a discussion that, in reality, never has "no" for an answer. For example if the response to the funding question is "no," it presents an opportunity to follow up with a question that invariably has a "yes" answer: "If your system/product failed today, is there funding available to repair it?"

Unless you're selling service on something that has no practical use, the answer is typically "yes." The response usually goes like this: "In that case I can draw from my expense budget or emergency fund." That opens up a discussion that can go in different directions depending on the situation. You may highlight the need to eliminate unplanned expenses, the ability to prevent problems by maintaining the equipment, or possibly the need to allocate funds from the expense budget to purchase service. Regardless of the situation, it must be determined if there is funding available to purchase your service.

The best-case scenario would be to come away knowing the amount available. This information is vital when preparing the proposal. One method of gaining insight into available funding is attempting to find out how much has been spent on service this year and over the past few years. This gives insight not only into currently available funding but also into important trends in spending. The bottom line is you can't sell something to someone who has no money. Many of us who claim otherwise as we dig into our wallets to grab our favorite vanity credit cards, but businesses typically don't operate this way. Without, "F" you don't have a qualified prospect.

- **Authority**

Once again we revisit the decision maker and sponsor topic. The goal is to identify and qualify the person who will authorize the service agreement. This individual is typically the decision maker, but in some cases the person actually authorizing the agreement may be different. In almost all cases sponsors *don't* authorize service agreements. They recommend, cheer on, promise to help you, and present themselves in ways that may lead you to believe they authorize the agreement. Don't be fooled. This error is the leading cause of lost sales.

Not identifying and speaking or meeting with the person who will ultimately make the final decision is the primary factor in over 30 percent of lost service agreement proposals. It's not unusual to meet with someone and determine he is the correct person based on any number of factors. Title, system/product knowledge, and relationship with end users are often used as justification by service salespeople for not asking the direct question: "Are you the person who will be authorizing the purchase of a service agreement on the equipment?" It sounds simple enough, but far too many service salespeople would rather take a walk on the wild side and sidestep the question.

For example you're calling on a clinic with the intention of selling a service agreement on piece of mammography equipment. The appointment is with the head of radiology, who purchased the equipment and is listed as the point of contact in company records. The person tells you he is responsible for maintaining the equipment. There is even a budget established for system maintenance in his department. It would be easy to assume you have the authorizing party. Unfortunately, after not getting a timely decision on the agreement, you dig deeper and find out the proposal is on the administrator's desk. This could be due to a number of reasons including:

- The department head only has the authority to approve expense items.
- Purchases over $10,000 must have higher levels of approval.
- All contracts must be reviewed by legal, purchasing, HQ, etc., which is coordinated through the administrator's office.
- The head of radiology is an MD who would never admit not to have authority for anything!

Determining your contact is the authorizing party should not be left to an educated guess or a chance. This is not a case of rolling the dice. This is a case of professionally qualifying the prospect. Never conclude a call anything less than certain you have made contact with the person or persons who will authorize the purchase of your proposal.

- **Need**

Analyzing the needs of potential clients is fundamental to sales. There are countless books and articles on the subject. Most of the companies I work with have developed service offerings that provide solutions to the perceived needs of their target markets. In many cases these solutions have been developed over time and have seen little change.

All too often market needs don't align with current service offerings. In a perfect world needs and offerings would align. I will assume for the sake of this discussion your company has a well-defined set of offerings that allow you to meet the needs of all your customers. If this is the case, congratulations! If not, use your imagination.

Obviously the N in WFAN is focused on determining the needs of your client. This is done by gaining insight via questioning, data regarding the specific equipment, or regulatory requirements.

My experience tells me there is an almost equal split between objective needs based on the above and subjective needs based on the individual perspectives, quirks, and experiences of the prospect. For many clients these needs far outweigh the traditional set of broad-based needs that are common across a similar client base. Sometimes these needs are stated clearly by the prospect. If not you may need to stir the pot to get them to surface.

I would like to claim all of my sales were the results of my superior skills. In reality many just fell in my lap due to the lack of performance by my competition. I was always fortunate to work for companies that had great service cultures and fostered high customer-satisfaction levels. I would like to say this is the norm for most technology-based product-service providers, but that is not always the case. Service delivery tends to slip in lagging economies as workforce reductions are the norm and training budgets are cut.

Oftentimes, when the installation market is thriving, technicians are borrowed from service to complete jobs. Regardless of the reason, I've sold many service agreements due primarily to the shortcomings of others. Most of the problems were related to the lack of technical support provided by my competitors, but often other areas were the targets of my clients' wrath. Listed below are some of the subjective needs of clients I've heard while participating in qualifying calls that ultimately generated sales. Once again these were shortcomings of their current service providers.

- Invoice doesn't give enough information—just a line item.
- Technician showed up an hour late—I missed my tee time.
- No one to talk to—calls almost always goes to voicemail.
- Every time I call for service I have to speak with a different person.

- Technicians show up unannounced.
- I'm tired of telling their guy to park his truck behind the building.
- They keep forcing me to buy multi-year contracts.
- I don't trust them. I never see them around the building.
- They send a new technician every time.
- I think they're an arrogant company.

Once you hear any of the above reasons for customer dissatisfaction, things tend to proceed in a positive way. Every one of these complaints typically makes it easy to differentiate and sell the performance of your company:

"We're customer focused."

"Communicating with our customers is a priority."

"Our technicians have completed a customer service course."

One or all of these statements are usually worked into the conversation to satiate the prospect. As for objective needs, almost all clients have similar needs regarding response time, maintenance schedules, cost, etc. Consider yourself lucky when one of the above quirky needs surface.

Just like W, F, and A, it is an absolute requirement to walk away with N established. Don't fall into the trap of telling the prospect what his needs are. This is a common shortcoming of mediocre service salespeople. They're so good at their jobs they don't even bother to ask their prospects what most concerns them. They know everything from their experiences calling on similar clients. "Mr. Client, let me tell you what we provide." If this statement is conveyed before you've made every attempt to have the prospect open up and discuss his situation, you need to stop! This is a case of knowing what you sell and not what your prospect may need.

Summary

I contend the major difference between failing, mediocre, and overachieving service sales representatives is the ability to qualify their prospects. Many make judgments to proceed to the next step in the sales cycle without enough information. One of the main reasons for this is a lack of discipline. We tend to overestimate our skills and fall into bad habits.

Selling is a process. Much of that process is solely determined and controlled by the salesperson. Many jobs are process focused. Watch a pilot conduct a preflight check, a batter prepare to step into the box, or a band do a sound check. All are well-developed processes. A service salesperson's process goes beyond the sales cycle. Each step within the cycle has its own process. When it comes to qualifying, it's all about WFAN. Write those letters at the top of your notepad. Make sure you gain the necessary information to satisfy each letter. It will not only make you more effective; it will also make you more efficient. Qualify, qualify, quality!

Chapter 6

SURVEY
SEE THE FOREST AND THE TREES

The well-known proverb "can't see the forest for the trees" references people who put too much emphasis on details and often lose sight of the larger picture. Surprisingly this statement is found in writings dated in the 1500s.

The counterpoint is "can't see the trees for the forest." This refers to individuals who typically see the bigger picture while overlooking smaller details. Which statement applies to you? Do you look at a potential client as a great opportunity while overlooking potential obstacles? Or do you put too much emphasis on the obstacles and lose sight of the bigger opportunity? Regardless of your perspective, your questions should be: How does this proverb apply to selling service? And what relevance does it have when conducting a survey for a potential service agreement?

The majority of service agreement proposals are prepared after completing surveys. Rarely is it possible to generate a solid proposal for a service agreement without knowing what equipment will be covered. Not only do you need an accurate inventory of the equipment, but additional information is required to create a proposal that is based on a rational cost estimate. Inadequate surveys lead to bad estimates that usually result in bad proposals.

Ironically some of these proposals will turn into sales as clients happily purchase service agreements that were underpriced by the salesperson. All too often customers receive too much value based on their actual situations. The customer wins, and the salesperson may win depending on his compensation plan, but the company most often will lose. Typically the service department suffers the most from underfunded agreements as they consume more material and manpower than estimated. This is one of the primary reasons stress between sales and service is present in almost all companies. The others being sales personnel's habits of over-committing service delivery schedules or equipment performance.

Survey requirements vary widely by the product or system being pursued for service. Size and complexity are key factors when deciding if an onsite survey is required or if the information in hand is enough to generate a proposal. Consideration must also be given to the cost of traveling to the site by the salesperson. Knowledge and familiarity with the equipment must also be taken into account.

Another major factor is how the equipment is applied. Standalone devices often found in the medical-equipment, business-product, and capital-equipment markets usually have standard applications and specifications. Products that are integrated or customized, typical of the building and process-controls markets, need closer examination as their applications vary by installation.

Often the bill of materials in company files doesn't match what is actually at the client site. This is due to the moves, adds, and changes to the building and system that are not recorded during the installation and over time. The situation can also become more complicated when the installation of the equipment was done by others and up-to-date information is not communicated to the vendor or client.

The requirement to perform a survey varies by company. The goal of the potential service provider is to develop a proposal that meets the company's financial expectations, minimizes risk, and generates a sale. The goal of the salesperson is to present to the client a value proposition he can't refuse. The goal of the customer is to purchase a service agreement at the lowest price possible. And don't overlook the goal of the service department: to receive as much revenue as possible so they can provide the resources to support the agreement.

Obviously there's a great potential for any one of these constituencies to be disappointed. The quality of the survey impacts all parties.

If you're selling service on equipment that requires only a model number available in company records to generate a proposal, consider yourself lucky. For many service salespeople the survey is not a welcomed experience. It may require a large block of time—hours or even days. It may be necessary to change out of business dress and into clothes that can withstand the rigors of working in close proximity to dirt, grime, and uncomfortable environmental conditions. Often the need for ear protection, goggles, shoe covers, and protective clothing are OSHA (Occupational Safety and Health Administration) or client requirements.

Some surveys require working at heights that may raise the pulse level. Areas where people or animals are in distress can generate negative emotional responses that only service salespeople made of stone could ignore. Building surveys can be adventures as you observe the behind-the-scenes activities of wide-ranging enterprises. While some adventures can be exhilarating, others can be harrowing. It's a personal experience. Looking back there are surveys still fresh in my mind decades later.

Bad:
- Prisons. Walking through cell blocks is not a pleasant experience. In particular women's prisons if you're a male or vice versa if you're a female. Not only was it

depressing to see people behind bars, but the comments they sent my way robbed me of any innocence I'd once had. A young guy walking around in a suit escorted by a guard is hard to miss. Of course the guard would tell me to ignore them. Oh yeah, like I wasn't trying that method! Only minutes earlier I'd been listening to (and probably singing along with) some tunes on my car radio. Now I was being referred to as "meat" and other consumables. It didn't matter if I toured high or minimum-security prisons. I always departed scared straight.

- Roofs. In my early years of working for Honeywell, I had to conduct many surveys on building roofs as that was where equipment related to commercial air conditioning is often located. I'm not a fan of high places to say the least. My heart starts to race and it takes every ounce of my energy not to flee. Anything over a few stories and I'm at risk. Walking on top of a sixty-story office building in windy Chicago, a sun-baked condo tower in Miami, or a casino hotel during an ice storm in Atlantic City are a few of the many experiences I would like to forget.

- Hospitals. I don't have any fears regarding hospitals. I'm fortunate in that the sights, sounds, and smells typical of health-care facilities don't bother me—with one exception. Children's hospitals. Each and every one was a heartbreaking experience. Within minutes I would feel my overall demeanor change, and my ability to conduct my work diminished.

I thought I'd seen it all until I visited a huge children's hospital in Russia. I was with a team of facility professionals visiting Moscow in the '90s. We were advising operators of large facilities on ways to organize their staff and develop budgets in the "new" Russia. I saw countless young children literally jammed into rooms, bed touching bed, at least six kids in rooms designed for two. As for sanitary conditions, think of an interstate highway restroom that hasn't been cleaned in a couple of weeks during the peak summer season, and the air conditioning is out of order. I lasted about ten minutes, then returned to our bus and shed a few tears.

- Manufacturing plants. Many plants are noisy, hot, and not the cleanest environments. I'm not speaking of the high-tech, clean-room facilities but the places where they actually make stuff you find in hardware, discount, and auto-parts stores.

  The hardest thing to deal with was the air quality. I wore contact lenses for most of my life. Within minutes of walking into some of these facilities, I would feel them harden as they became saturated with irritants in the air. If it wasn't my eyes it was my nose, as allergic reactions would quickly develop.

  I recall a situation surveying a chemical plant in New Jersey that led to my nose bleeding multiple times that evening. I can only wonder how these environments impacted the health of the people who worked in these conditions for large parts of their lives. Many of the noise issues were eliminated with the introduction of ear protection. The introduction of goggles also had a positive impact. As for the spaces that contained massive boilers generating heat that would make a mannequin sweat, I may have lost a pound or two in these situations. Climbing around a boiler room in a blue suit, a tie, and a long-sleeve shirt in a temperature of over a hundred degrees will make anyone lose their cool.

Good:
- Bunkers. I had the opportunity to conduct surveys in a few underground bunkers. These low-key, unmarked facilities were designed for use as operation centers for major

companies should the unthinkable happen. Visits to these sites would include either long elevator rides or walking down numerous flights of stairs into reinforced chambers that had their own environmental-control systems, food supplies, dormitories, and other necessities to house a few dozen people for extended periods of time. All of them had the big electronic map that provided information for planning purposes as well as numerous monitors receiving news broadcasts from across the world. They were the closest things in real life to a James Bond set. Very cool indeed, but I was never offered a martini, shaken or stirred.

- Playboy clubs. Three. Enough said.
- Food processing plants. Potato chips, pretzels, chocolates, ice cream, pastries, candy of various types, alcohol, etc. "Would you like to try some? Or would you like to take some home with you?" Two of my all-time favorite questions.
- Manufacturing plants. There were the bad experiences mentioned above, but there were far more good ones. Those of you who enjoy the show *How Things Are Made* would love these places. For those of you who don't enjoy seeing raw material turned into finished products, you're missing something. I'm not even going to try to list the things I've seen manufactured, but if you've ever eaten, traveled, medicated, slept, read, exercised, or put on clothes, I've probably seen the stuff you've used being made.

Now back to the subject at hand: the survey step in the sales cycle and the before-mentioned proverb. Hopefully the survey is conducted *after* the prospect has been qualified. If you're doing surveys to create proposals for unqualified prospects, go back and read the previous chapter. Surveys take valuable sales time. They shouldn't be done gratuitously or to meet the expectations of others. For those of you who have, like I have, conducted surveys of large public-school districts that required crawling around dozens of buildings over multiple days in the hope of winning competitive bids against a myriad of competitors and lost, forget about it. Let's go back to the forest and the trees as a way to review what information needs to be collected during a survey. For the purpose of inclusiveness, I will assume a survey is being conducted on a system or an integrated piece of equipment.

Trees (Details)

- Equipment. A detailed list of the equipment to be maintained is an absolute requirement. It should include the part numbers of major devices, the age of the equipment to be maintained, and anything that interfaces with it. This information is of particular importance so the proposal can be configured to communicate clearly who is responsible for problems with equipment connected to the system being evaluated. A good example is a fire alarm system, which can interface with elevators, HVAC, lighting, central-station monitoring, emergency power supplies, and other life-safety systems.

  Needless to say accurate counts and amounts are helpful if not required. In some cases it's almost impossible to ascertain the exact amount of devices connected to large systems. In these situations the service agreement should include a term and condition that allows for additions to be made to the agreement if, upon inspection, a substantial amount of new devices are uncovered.

- Access. Eventually a service technician will need access to the equipment. Access means not only being able to enter the physical location but also having the hours available to work on the system or equipment. Most facilities want to minimize disruptions for their occupants or processes. Taking equipment offline for maintenance or repair has to be scheduled with the client. This can add additional cost if after-hours service is required or if only a portion of the equipment can be worked on at one time. Good examples would be elevators, escalators, HVAC, medical equipment, office equipment, and communications systems.

- Location
  - Facility—The location of the facility is important when determining travel time for both planned and unplanned service. The primary factor is the time required for technicians to reach the site during normal and after-hour work schedules. Some companies provide guidance for the service salesperson by creating formulas that include labor and travel charges based on their local office locations and other factors. Often technicians are not housed near company offices and work out of their homes. Many are required to cover vast territories that can encompass multiple cities, counties, states, and even countries. Regardless of the logistics, cost and response-time commitments are factors that need to be evaluated.

    Traffic patterns, travel expenses, weather, security clearance, and parking should all be taken into consideration as well. A good barometer is asking occupants about any issues related to traveling to the site like congested traffic periods.
  - System/product—There's nothing more frustrating for a busy technician than arriving at a site and not being able to gain access to the equipment requiring service. It's frustrating not only for the technician but also for the customer. Difficulty in locating the person

with the keys to the equipment closet, wing, room, etc., or finding out the equipment is thirty feet in the air and it's not specified which party provides the lift, can frustrate or anger everyone involved. The same goes for arriving at a site and finding it closed for a plant vacation shutdown.

- Problems. For many products and systems, the survey reveals problems visible via system diagnostics, trouble lights, or even audible alarms. Needless to say a product or system that is not currently operating is a problem, but it can also present an opportunity. It's probably the reason a service salesperson was contacted or granted the appointment in the first place.

This is always a welcomed situation by service salespeople, especially when the equipment is critical to the operation of the client's business or if an outside agency has mandated it be repaired. This is also a good example of why an onsite survey usually trumps researching a database or receiving information over the phone.

The question that must be asked before presenting a solution is, "What caused the problem?" Problems can often be disguised as product or system issues when in reality they occurred due to human or application issues. Another major problem area is Mother Nature. She can wreak havoc on electronics-based systems, creating power surges and other damage from severe weather. In cases where the system is not operating, a repair is usually required before a maintenance agreement can be sold.

Some service salespeople get creative and include the repair as part of the agreement to sweeten the offer. All too often the sale is made but the service department gets stuck with a bad situation—the problem repeatedly surfaces and they are on the hook to do the repair at no charge. Often the only way to eliminate the problem or reduce the risk of its reoccurrence is upgrading or adding hardware or software at no cost to the client while eroding supplier margins and profits.

A good example of this situation is when lightning suppression is added to a system. There's little doubt it can reduce the damage that can occur from a strike, but there are no guarantees. All service agreements should have an act of God clause, but when lightning protection is installed as part of a service agreement (not recommended) rather than a one-time sale, the terms and conditions found in most maintenance agreements can be left to interpretation.

In the case of an operator-created problem, training is often the solution, not a maintenance agreement. If the operator is not properly trained, the problem will almost always reappear. Products and systems that are not functioning due to misapplication need close scrutiny. If the application is potentially creating the problem, the service salesperson needs to get someone from operations involved to review the situation. Once again it's much easier to identify these issues when conducting an onsite survey.

Forest (Big Picture)

Often the information gathered during a survey regarding the broader situation is as important as—or even more important than—the required system information. A service salesperson needs to be all eyes and ears when visiting a site. Asking questions of equipment users or building occupants usually provides valuable insight into problems. Additionally these conversations may supply great information about the client, the business, or other vendors. An innocent question posed to an unsuspecting individual usually brings an honest response. I'm not saying a client may sometimes lie or try to deceive a service salesperson, but—well, actually, I am.

- Business. Is the parking lot full? Are occupants complaining about staff reductions or potential layoffs? Is the company making money? What is the occupancy level?
- Facility. Questions posed directly to occupants usually return great results. Is the building too hot or cold? Is the elevator ever out of order? Does the copy machine ever jam? Does the fire alarm ever go off? Is there a long wait to have an MRI? Some other things to look for: Is a competitor's service truck parked outside? Does the ceiling or floor have water damage? Are there any signs of vandalism? A new addition is planned for the building. Do your salespeople know about it?
- Politics. Is your client really the decision maker or is she in reality a sponsor? Is the client in good standing with her superior? Does she have any pet peeves you can use to your advantage? How do things actually get done?

The list of potential questions is limitless. That can also be said for the useful information that may be revealed during the survey. A good survey can help identify the right offer to present, but it can also garner other information that can help support a sale.

Methodology

The complexity of the system, age, manufacturer, condition, current problems, and the need for an accurate list of equipment are usually the factors considered when choosing a survey strategy. A word not often associated with surveys is *strategy*. The survey step in the sales process is part of the total strategy.

All too often this is not the case for many of my new clients. The survey can be overlooked when plotting an effective sales strategy. This oversight costs companies sales, lost profits from bad agreements, and lost revenue from missed repair or upgrade opportunities. Let's not forget the lost productivity of both service salespeople and operations staff.

Surveys cost time and money. In most situations it's a case of "pay me now or pay me later." Overlooked critical information could have led to a sale or generated a more accurate estimate of labor and materials required to perform the service. Some typical survey considerations are listed below.

- *When?* Surveys can be conducted before, immediately after, or some time following a first call. Time required onsite and additional travel time and expense for a separate trip are the major determining factors. In most cases the best scenario is to conduct the survey immediately after the qualifying call. Requesting the decision maker accompany you on the survey or direct you to the right person to assist in the survey adds credibility to the situation. Conducting the survey at the conclusion of the first call also adds a sense of urgency and provides the opportunity to point out any deficiencies. Immediate surveys also can shorten the sales cycle, significantly reduce sales costs, and improve a service sales representative's productivity.

- *How?* For most technology-based products, the survey is as simple as walking up to the equipment and recording the necessary information. For service agreements on systems that can extend to every part of a facility—like HVAC, building controls, or lighting—a thorough walk of the building is required. Numerous devices like sensors, pull stations, smoke detectors, and thermostats are located throughout the building.

Technology has had a major impact on survey efficiency over the years. Early in my career, I would return to my office and conduct what looked like a game of pantomime while trying to describe to my service manager what I'd seen. "It was about this big, red, some water was dripping from it, and I think it had both a wire and a pipe going into it."

Fortunately cheap, throwaway cameras eliminated the need for my one-act plays. Unfortunately I would have to wait a few days for the shots to be developed. Today digital-camera or cell-phone photos have expedited the process. When presenting a proposal, a good photo of a piece of equipment in need of service can have a great impact. Another useful item is a survey form. Some companies provide their salespeople with software that can be utilized to input data while conducting a survey. Often a simple hard copy form that outlines the needed information will suffice. Having to return to a site, make follow-up phone calls, or send e-mails to get needed information is avoidable if a salesperson has a good survey form that notes all the items that need to be addressed.

- *What?* Beyond collecting the counts and amounts needed to prepare an estimate, this is also the time to observe the overall condition of the equipment. For example when surveying a fire alarm system a major factor in keeping the system operating as designed is the need for clean smoke detectors. Smoke-detector chambers attract dust and other contaminants from the air that can generate false alarms. Particle buildup is normal, and typically an annual cleaning will reduce unwanted false alarms.

What can't be determined by looking at drawings or a bill of materials is the environment in which they are located. Areas that are exposed to chemicals, manufacturing processes, or a lack of building maintenance can require much more attention, thus impacting the labor estimate. A thorough survey will also reveal issues regarding access, as variables like ceiling height, locked entry points, and even hazardous environments are usually observed while walking the building.

In reality some facilities are just dirtier than others. This is true across almost all market segments. It's not unusual to walk into an office-building lobby that has eye-popping appeal, but beyond that point the rest of the facility looks like a set from the movie *Nine to Five*— which was made in 1980. I've seen million-dollar medical equipment used as a place to rest coffee cups, control panel closets relegated to the role of storage units filled with combustible items, and air conditioning and heating vents blocked by furniture and grime that has reduced the airway to a fraction of its capacity.

Often the most revealing information is uncovered during brief discussions with equipment operators. It's not unusual to meet people operating the equipment who have skills and experience equal to or exceeding the technicians the service company will provide. Sometimes this can be a good situation, as these people will only call for service when they can't solve the problem themselves. On the other hand, they can also fall into the Nutty Professor category as they push the equipment or systems beyond design parameters. They are usually easy to identify when you hear a sentence beginning with, "I reprogrammed it to..." Still, I prefer these individuals over the "I just hit it with a hammer when it acts up" guys

Surveys of building systems and standalone equipment should always start at the control panel—the heart and soul of the system. A control panel may be integrated directly into the piece of equipment. It can also stand alone, nearby, or remotely containing hardware and software. Control panels can range in size from a full room (nuclear power plant) to a simple touchpad (copy machine).

Most standalone control panels are locked. I would estimate about 50 percent of the time you can reach on top of the panel and locate the key, though it may require disturbing the spider using it as a bed. Often jammed into the conduit near the panel is a set of schematics or even an equipment list that may be of great help. It's also not unusual to see a sticker affixed to the panel with the name of the current service provider or even the date of the last service.

When opening the panel, a great indicator of the service history is the battery. Many control panels have batteries as backup power supplies should there be a failure with the primary electrical system. Almost all batteries have information regarding the date they were installed. If you're looking at a five-year-old battery, chances are the system has not been maintained.

Special attention needs to be taken when surveying systems or equipment provided by someone other than your company. These situations provide additional risk as familiarity with the product, system condition, parts availability, software programming, etc. may be outside the comfort zone of your technical staff. In some situations service companies are called upon by clients who know their product is in distress or have been notified by their current provider that parts or software are no longer available. In short if the client contacts you to provide a proposal for service on equipment that was not provided by your company, there is usually a back-story, so beware. In many cases the client will not be forthcoming with the reason he is entertaining proposals. You and your company may be set up to fail. Qualifying these situations is extremely important. Conducting time-consuming surveys that are long shots at best is not recommended.

Summary

At the heart of every service agreement for products or systems is the equipment being covered. For many standalone pieces of equipment, the survey is a simple step that may only require a product or serial number. All the information regarding the equipment is available in company files or databases.

For those selling service on systems customized for each facility, the survey step in the sales cycle requires more effort and has greater importance. Regardless of the situation, the goal is the same: gather the necessary information that will allow you to develop an estimate that includes enough labor, materials, and other resources to support the service program being proposed. At the same time you need to provide a solution and value proposition that will motivate the client to buy and meet the financial requirements of your company. Overlooking important information during the survey can lead to an estimate that can cost a service salesperson a sale or generate a sale that will not meet client or company expectations.

Chapter 7

OFFER
THE AGE OF ENLIGHTENMENT

Fundamental to any sale is an offer made by the seller to the potential buyer. *Offer* in this context is the services proposed to the client. Some salespeople have little control over what's included in the offer as it's predetermined by the company they represent. Others have opportunities to configure offerings to meet their prospects' specific needs. The ability to tailor an offer can range from "whatever you want" to basic gold, silver, or bronze or singular options. The determining factor driving most offers is the product's service requirements. Other major considerations are the distribution channel and the logistics required to deliver the service. Firms that manufacture, sell, and provide service on products have a greater ability to control service delivery and configure offers. A primary advantage is their accessibility to parts and software. These direct-distribution models allow for more flexibility in the management of resources.

Companies that utilize multi-step distribution channels usually require their distributors to adhere to corporate guidelines regarding service. Even with the best intentions, they struggle to monitor the service quality of their distributors. On the other hand many distributors struggle to develop effective offerings due to limitations in their service-marketing expertise. Regardless of the channel or the scope of the services offered, service providers need to present prospects with solutions that provide value.

Services Provided

Service agreements, repairs, retrofits, upgrades, moves, adds, changes, inspections, testing, parts, warranties, service calls, emergency service, repair and exchange, software support, software upgrades, bug fixes, reporting, training, adjustments, cleaning, calibration, phone support, remote diagnostics, monitoring, audits, performance reviews, archiving, database management, help desks, blogs, and webinars are some of the services offered by service providers. Some of these services are proactive and minimize the chances of equipment failure. Some help clients service their own equipment or enhance its performance. Others are intended to respond to problems. All have been designed to meet the needs of customers who purchased products, systems, or software with the expectation they will need service support.

Coverage

Full, modified, gold, silver, bronze, premium, plus, enhanced, basic, premier, and preferred are just some of the labels companies use to describe their service offers. In all honesty I don't like any of them. Unfortunately they are common in the service industry. I've had many debates with major company executives and business owners who think by creating labels they have made it easier to market their services. They feel the prospective customer needs simplification to understand the differences in coverage levels. I guess that implies their customers aren't smart enough to know what they need and are relegated to second class, if not third class, if they have funding restrictions.

In my opinion no customer should ever be treated differently from another. The categorizing of customers negatively impacts a company's ability to build a service culture. Some companies contend it's easier for their salespeople to have limited service options than to create a service offering to meet each client's unique needs. There's no doubt it's easier, but it doesn't make it better for the customer.

I struggle with telling customers they are less important than another because they have not purchased the highest level of service offering. This is especially true when selling service agreements on mission-critical equipment:

"Help, our system is down and fifteen hundred people are standing in the parking lot in the rain!"

"I'm sorry, but because you only purchased our Lower Middle Bronze level of service, we can't come for a few hours."

I think these labels are created either to simplify order entry and processing due to limitations of a CRM system or because service marketing is run by someone with a product marketing background. Regardless, when it comes to service marketing, nothing beats offering a package of services that meet a specific customer's needs. End of story!

Terms and Conditions

Billing periods, renewals, escalations, indemnification clauses, vehicle charges, travel and living expenses, hours of operation, existing condition terms, disruption of operation clauses, uptime guarantees, vandalism clauses, and discounts are some of the items that typically are not visible but are very important to potential customers. Often their importance supersedes the actual services provided, especially to the client's legal, purchasing, and finance support staff. It would be great if we could present service agreements that didn't include reading-glasses-required information, but that's not realistic in today's litigious business world.

Sales Aids

The salesperson, technician, service agreement, sales brochure, data sheets, presentation folder, business card, PowerPoint presentation, Website, envelope, e-mail, letter, trade-show booth, and graphic treatments visible to the prospect are all part of the offer. All too often these items are overlooked and not taken seriously by service providers. One person may pay little attention to anything but the offering and the price while another may reject a proposal because there is a term or condition that confuses them. Some clients may be turned off by dated logos or print that's too small to read. All clients are turned off by service agreements that don't clearly explain what's being offered and the benefits they will enjoy if they purchase it.

One area I find most service providers overlooking is their Websites. Most have services displayed somewhere on their sites. Sometimes service is prominent and has simple navigation to good information. What I find with many smaller companies are Websites that are dated and don't present the needed information for potential service clients. Not surprisingly most sites are up to date and creative in the presentation of product information. All too often the service information has a "yes, we do service" or "customer satisfaction is our business" spin. Service is represented but it looks like an appendage to the products and systems business the company is so proud of.

Some of the hardest selling I do with clients is to update their Websites. Many feel their Websites are good enough as no one really purchases or makes buying decisions based on their sites. There is some merit to this position. Most companies that provide services on products don't generate revenue directly via the Internet. As for indirect impact, it's usually more than they're aware of. The companies that need to open their eyes fall into two categories:

1. Manufacturers—specifically companies that don't sell their products and systems directly to the end user. Often these buyers were not directly involved in selecting the product and seek information to help them source and

purchase service. This group could include equipment operators or decision makers that were not in their positions when the equipment was installed. They are information seekers—service information seekers. They couldn't care less about videos, slick photos, or overzealous claims about products. What they most often find is generic information or a dead end. A "Contact Us" page is not the solution for providing information.

2. Single-source providers. Many of my clients are extending their brands by marketing services that are adjacent to or synergistic with their traditional service offerings. Some provide single sourcing to add revenue. Others expand their services to fend off competition. In either case most prospective clients are not totally familiar with the company and go to their Website to review their capabilities before switching service providers. In some cases they will only spend a few minutes looking over the site to verify the company's existence, to get a sense of their overall capabilities, or just because it's the right thing to do. If a prospective client goes to the site and sees that service is not positioned at a proper level or that the overall look and feel of the site is not very professional, a great sales effort may be doomed. I'm not a fan of bloated, overdesigned Websites. Information needs to be easy to access and concise in content. The important thing is the right information needs to be available at the click of a button.

For the sake of discussion I will assume your company has allowed some level of flexibility in creating your service offering. If that's not the case, you have been relegated to selling a service product—a commodity. That makes it very difficult to differentiate your services from others' and makes selling service a boring job. It's hard to be creative and maximize your consultative selling skills when your offering is chosen from a menu with one item or from the choice of three value meals. If this is your situation service sales means discussing, defending, justifying, and analyzing one thing: price. I will also assume the prospect has been qualified, his needs have been analyzed, and an offer is being prepared that he can't refuse.

A service agreement can be sold as part of the initial bid submittal or at the time of purchase. It is often just a line item in a specification or presented as an extended warranty. Some companies promote this strategy as it eliminates the need to follow up on the sale and contact the client. This situation is very common when equipment is sold through an indirect distribution channel. Manufacturers want to ensure end users are presented with service options to support the operation of their equipment. They also want to ensure their distribution channel provides service agreements. The presold scenario has downside implications that are often overlooked. Not that I would ever cast negative comments at product salespeople, but they may forget or even discount the service agreement to get the equipment sale. I've even heard rumor that some product salespeople may include post-sale service free for a year, two, or until the Cubs win the World Series. Rumors—all rumors, of course.

Of concern are situations where the owner/operator of the system was not involved at the time of purchase. The end user didn't have a voice in making the equipment purchase or the service decision and may resent being locked in to a service agreement. Once again the ability to qualify the prospect and present the right offering is missed. All too often this leads to an unhappy customer and puts the service department in a no-win situation. In short, they have a dysfunctional relationship.

Many products and systems sold offer the opportunity to approach the customer to discuss service options during the installation. For example, the installation period for a building or process-control system could easily last a year. It's hard to get an individual to set aside the time to discuss a maintenance agreement when all that is visible is exposed girders or unoccupied space. It's also common that the product or system installed is reconfigured during the installation.

It's almost impossible to get a final snapshot of what is actually installed without a thorough visual survey. Job scopes change all the time in the construction industry. A person selling service needs to have an accurate list of equipment to develop a proposal. In such a situation the service salesperson should monitor the installation's progress and start the effort to identify the person who will be responsible for making the service purchase decision. Typically the picture becomes clear midway through the installation. Regardless of the situation contacting the right person sooner rather than later is always better.

Most often service agreements are pursued post-warranty. In most cases this is not the right strategy. Service options should be presented during the warranty period if not before. Most warranties only cover product failures. Service options like response times, after-hours coverage, and troubleshooting are not covered. The best answer is proposing a two-year agreement. The first year would provide service taking into account that parts replacement is covered under warranty. The second year's cost would reflect the price level moving forward. This allows the customer to set budget levels and ensure continuity of service. It also relieves the service provider from having to sell the service agreement a second time.

Speaking of warranties, who came up with the idea to extend warranties beyond a year? Two years? Five years? I think you probably know the answer. Yes, it was product marketing people. It was a no-brainer from their perspective. It immediately provided a competitive advantage. That was until everyone else started doing it. I'm sure solid estimates were done to reserve future dollars for the service department to deliver free service in those out years. Dream on! From a service provider or service marketing perspective, extended warranties may be the worst idea ever!

There's a long list of considerations that must be taken into account when creating a service offering. It requires reflecting back on the qualifying call and creating the perfect balance between needs and price. For well-trained service salespeople, this step is easy. If they did a spot-on job qualifying the prospect, the offering almost creates itself. For those who didn't nail WFAN, that failure becomes apparent at this point in the sales cycle.

My good friend and colleague, Greg Scott, refers to this process as *authoring*. He feels a good service salesperson becomes the author of a great offer. He also feels a great service salesperson is able to have the prospect coauthor the offering during the qualifying call. It makes perfect sense. If we feel a sense of ownership in something, it's highly likely we'll support it. It's much easier to close a sale in a coauthor situation.

Let's review some of the primary items that need to be considered when developing an offer.

- Cost: Service agreements come with a cost. Trained technicians are required, parts and software need repair, and the logistics of getting both to a site entail expenses that need to be addressed. Most clients would like to purchase the maximum coverage available but understand financial realities require negotiating the best agreements they can afford. Priorities need to be set and trade-offs are commonplace. Often salespeople get overzealous when clients demonstrate willingness to purchase the most inclusive agreements available. This usually leads to proposing solutions that will not be sold, or to discounting. Most clients are unwilling to restructure deals and salespeople don't want to prepare additional proposals. The solution is simple: qualify the prospect and make sure what your proposing is in line with the client's funding.

- Market segment: If you're selling your services to one market segment, its attributes become self-determining. A good example would be medical equipment. The level of usage may vary, but it's primarily sold to health-care providers. The same could be said for selling service on aircraft, drilling rigs, or military equipment. You know how the buyer uses the equipment, typically there is minimal competition, and service requirements are well defined.

Those selling service on products utilized in wide-ranging facilities and applications need to play close attention to each market's unique characteristics. Elevator service is a good example. Obviously elevators are found in multistory buildings. Some are used at high rates while others are used periodically. Some buildings have multiple units while in others there's a single unit for vertical transportation. Some are located in posh buildings that cater to their clientele while others may be in facilities where landlords don't have quite the same level of customer-care standards. Some facilities have their own technical staff while others may only have a custodian with little technical acumen.

Salespeople who service this market may walk into a half dozen different building types in a single day. They need to be sensitive to each facility's application and purchasing habits. Even in an industry, like elevators, that has code requirements for inspections, the service offering may vary widely. Response time is a good example. Do you think a Ritz-Carlton has the same response time requirement as Father Tim's Cheap Inn? Can Fred afford an agreement that includes all parts and labor? It's extremely important to treat each call and client individually when packaging an offer.

- Application: The way products or systems are applied also needs to be considered when formulating a service offering. Often a product can be integrated into another piece of equipment that can have a significant impact on its performance. Usage can also vary widely as operating cycles may have some equipment operating in short spans, limited hours, or environments that don't require excessive use.

On the other hand, the equipment may have been misapplied and may be operating at levels for which it was not designed. Simple applications usually warrant trouble-free operation and cost-effective service agreements for both the client and the vendor. As for those "bad boy" applications, building a service solution requires a thorough examination of the situation and great care when developing the service offering.

- Access: Service technicians need to have access to the equipment when service is required. If the product has remote access capability, then this isn't a problem. For the majority of service salespeople this is a major issue. When will technicians be able to work on the equipment? Will advance scheduling be required? Will the client need to provide a staff member to observe or escort the person? Do service technicians need special security clearance or protective clothing? Can the service vehicle find convenient parking or will it have to be left in a no-parking zone? These are just a few issues that may need to be considered while preparing your service offering.
- Codes and standards: For some service salespeople the core of the service agreement isn't negotiable. Local, state, or federal agencies may have determined what service offering is required. Inspection and

maintenance schedules are driven by codes that may not be overlooked. In most cases clients may incur legal or financial penalties if they don't perform the required services. These situations appear to require less creativity and consideration.

In reality this is typically not the case. Highly regulated situations usually breed competition from lower cost service providers that adhere to the required service requirements but don't provide other needed services. This can put solution-oriented providers at a disadvantage if they aren't able to differentiate themselves and demonstrate their value. I have spent a large part of my service marketing career helping companies in the life-safety services industry package service solutions that encompass more than the minimum standards required. Most struggle to differentiate themselves and far too often respond by lowering themselves to the levels of their competitors rather than properly marketing their value propositions.

- Equipment age: Almost all systems and products have life cycles. Every time a system is used it's one cycle closer to its mechanical or technological limit. A key criterion when packaging a service solution is determining where the equipment is in its life cycle. Obviously, new equipment is less likely to need repair and replacement. Mature equipment may work fine with a good maintenance program. Old equipment may already be defying the odds and still be operating beyond its useful life.

Offering full-service agreements that include fixed prices for parts and labor on old equipment may not be the logical solution from a cost perspective for the client or the service provider. The client knows it, your company knows it, and you know it, so don't offer them.

Positioning the Offer

Often even the best salespeople overlook positioning the service offering in the best way possible with the potential customer. Even a plain-vanilla offering needs to be presented in a fashion that relates to the specific prospect's needs. As no two clients physically look alike (except identical twins), no two prospects are motivated by the same purchase criteria. If properly qualified the prospect's specific or unique needs should surface.

Underachieving salespeople often treat everyone the same. They present the same package of services over and over without consideration for the individuality of the client. I'm not speaking in this section about creating a customized offering. I'm speaking about highlighting the services, terms, or other considerations on which the particular client places value. One person may place a high value on utilizing factory-certified technicians while another puts more value on quick response while another believes documentation of all service activities is at the top of the list. It's not what's important to the salesperson or the company; it's all about the client.

With that said a critical part in the sales cycle is enlightening the prospect about the maintenance requirements of his system or product. We often assume the client is educated on what is required so we don't give this element of the call proper attention. Let's be honest: no one really wants to be sold anything. They want to buy what they need. It's the job of a service salesperson to enlighten the prospect about what's needed to keep the equipment operating at peak efficiency. It's my belief that if this is done properly a rational person will do the right thing and purchase the services recommended.

On the other hand telling the client what she needs may not make her a buyer. To enlighten is provide knowledge or insight. The person who receives this enlightenment comes to an educated decision based on information she processes internally. It's the service salesperson's job to provide this information in a style that is informative, not condescending or argumentative. A good example would be a discussion regarding the present condition and age of a prospect's equipment and its potential failure or cost of replacement. I've been part of far too many sales calls where the prospect is proud to convey that his system has been operating fine and the salesperson I'm traveling with ignores the facts. The salesperson usually shifts into the "call me when you need me" or "I'll ignore what you just said" mode. The fact is the system is approaching a point in its life cycle where, yes, it is operating as designed, but things may start to fail and interrupt the system's performance. It's not time to scare the client into action. It's time to enlighten the prospect about the fact that over the coming months the situation can change without warning. He needs some facts or examples that will educate him without making him feel he is being intimidated or threatened.

Value Proposition

A much written about and important marketing term is *value proposition*. The creation of a value proposition is usually central to a company's business strategy for products and services sold. Supporting the concept is the need to create service offerings clients will judge to have value after analyzing their benefits and costs. If the prospects don't perceive value, they will not make purchases in almost all cases.

If we conclude value = benefits - cost being equal to zero or greater, we should make a sale. So why do so many proposals go unsold even when we present strong cases? I'm not a math expert, but it's easy to recognize one of the elements in this equation is subjective while the other two are not.

Let's start with cost. Even when manipulated by discounting or just pulled out of the air, it's clearly stated in dollars and cents. A $13,150 service agreement is exactly that. It doesn't matter if this number came off a price list, was generated by an estimating system, or was negotiated. At the end of the day, someone will be paying this amount.

Benefits are not as black and white but are visible in the agreement. They are usually outlined in the proposal and highlighted in sales aids. Parts are included or not, the number of inspections is listed, maintenance tasks are outlined, parts discounts are noted, etc. Of course there is room for interpretation by either party, but we'll overlook that for the sake of this discussion.

When it comes to quantifying value, it's almost impossible. Like beauty, value is in the eye of the beholder. It's personal, subjective, and refuses to be quantified in most cases. It doesn't apply itself to the rules of logic or any known mathematical formula or calculation, including the one mentioned in the previous paragraph. It's usually based on the prospect's personal experiences, good and bad. Often the client has a predetermined position regarding value and may be unwilling to alter her perception. What can a service salesperson do to overcome this significant obstacle to closing a sale? How can you get a prospect to understand and believe what you're proposing is a great value when she thinks otherwise?

My answer is accept the situation and work with it. In a perfect world, the prospect would think the services you are proposing are worth the amount you are charging. Even better she may think you are charging too little. In either case this is the outcome we are seeking. We want the prospect to believe she is getting the most for her money. This is easy to accomplish when you undercharge or offer profit-margin busting discounts. Normally that business strategy doesn't last too long.

The best method is to present a service agreement that's in line with what the prospect wants and fulfills the service requirements of the equipment. The agreement needs to be customer-centric, not service-provider-centric. Far too many companies create service offerings cast in concrete with little room for customization. Some think creating a few service levels will solve the problem. They would solve the problem if the world weren't composed of individuals who take pride in their abilities to make educated decisions for themselves and their companies. Presenting a proposal that doesn't reflect the needs of the prospect and his funding situation or that fails to present a value proposition to the actual decision maker usually doesn't sell. Once again it's all about qualifying.

Services

Companies offer services clients need. People purchase service agreements and receive services. So what are these services? Why do clients need them? Why can't we make products and systems that don't need service? Is it true companies make products that break so they can sell us expensive services?

I'm not going to get into a discussion about all the reasons why the service industry is the fastest growing segment of most economies around the globe, or about why stuff breaks. In most cases the services offered fall into one or a combination of the following offerings.

- Testing: Periodic, scheduled testing to ensure systems are operating as designed. It usually uncovers deficiencies that need attention. People purchase testing agreements to prevent system or product breakdowns. In some cases it's difficult to justify testing as the equipment may be in constant use, in essence self-testing.

Testing is often mandated by authorities who require systems be periodically tested to ensure public safety. Often companies try to differentiate themselves by attempting to communicate they do more thorough jobs of testing than competitors, utilize highly trained individuals, or perform the tests on schedule. Often the client is responsive to these assurances, but this is not always the case.

If not positioned correctly the prospect may perceive testing as a commodity with little to distinguish one provider from another except price. Selling testing-only agreements is not a service solution. Even when mandated, testing is the minimum requirement. It isn't a solution to maintain the system in proper working condition.

- Inspection: Similar to testing, inspections may be requirements or options. A test usually involves interaction with the product or system to verify it will perform as required. An inspection typically involves observing the system to see if it's installed as designed and if there are any apparent obstructions to its operation when needed. For example, it wouldn't be prudent to test a fire-sprinkler system by letting water flow into a workspace. The best approach is to inspect each sprinkler head to see if it is damaged or obstructed and if there is sufficient water available should it be called upon. Similar to testing, inspections are not service solutions. They are just tasks that need to be performed.

- Maintenance: Preventive maintenance programs are proactive services that address problems before they occur. Problems may be uncovered based on testing or inspection of the equipment. Also common is maintenance based on predictions of potential issues related to the equipment's age and usage. Predictive maintenance programs are most commonly presented by the equipment manufacturer or installer, as they have the information and data needed to forecast maintenance tasks. Maintenance programs typically provide the best means for limiting problems with equipment. They are usually expensive, as they are labor intensive. When positioned properly clients are responsive and perceive the value in maintaining their products. On the other hand, there is still a segment of the market that doesn't perceive the value of maintenance programs and sees break-fix as the most economical solution.

- Parts replacement: Sooner or later minor and major components of any product or system will fail. Most fail due to normal usage and aging. Often the damage is due to electrical issues or misuse. Service agreements that include the cost of parts replacement may vary from partial to full coverage. Many companies will include parts at no charge if they are below a certain cost ceiling, even when parts coverage is not included. In almost all cases failure beyond normal wear and tear, including weather-related issues, electrical strikes, and vandalism, are not included in parts-replacement coverage.

The most common coverage includes repair or replacement of like parts and not upgrades. In cases where parts are no longer manufactured or available, they are excluded from replacement coverage. An issue that always seems to arise is the customer who thinks he will have a system forever if he has purchased parts coverage, especially if he's had it for a number of years. The best way to ensure the customer understands what is and what is not covered is clear terms and conditions. I find many companies fall short in this area.

Parts coverage usually adds a significant cost to a service agreement, especially when coverage is provided on a system that is well beyond its warranty period. The clients who are most responsive to parts coverage are seeking the ability to set annual budgets for equipment maintenance and not take the risk of having to find funds for unplanned expenditures. By the way there is no reason annual limits can't be incorporated into the agreement. Like all other offerings, parts replacement doesn't have to be an all-or-nothing proposition.

- Software support: Very few users are willing to take risks and see their software become obsolete or not operating as intended. Most clients recognize the need for software agreements. They accept the fact that software may have issues, needs to be maintained, and evolves over time. They experience these same issues in their personal lives and with other systems that are part of their businesses.

The most common shortcoming of providers is offering generic software-support agreements. They all tend to look the same. There needs to be more creativity in this area, especially by involving clients in software performance and development. When it comes to software support, clients can be part of the solution, not just service consumers.

- Repair labor: Usually labor to replace failed parts or correct software issues is included with parts or software-support coverage. The system fails, the technician sources the solution and fixes it, and there is no charge. On occasion I've seen firms that differentiate between the troubleshooting time to locate the problem and the actual time to fix it. I'm not a big supporter of this approach as it leaves too much room for interpretation when it comes to charges that will be billed to the client. As with parts coverage, this offering is most appealing to clients who want to pay one annual, fixed amount.

- Service calls: Most clients don't like to pay invoices for service calls, especially those that are after hours or only require quick fixes. They think overtime charges are too high and they don't understand why they are charged for two hours when a technician was only onsite for fifteen minutes. Labor charges, vehicle or trip charges, and gas surcharges are commonly added to invoices and add up quickly.

Billing for service calls generates high levels of customer complaints and dissatisfaction. It also adds administrative time to settle disputes. Many service providers are reluctant to bill important clients for after-hours charges while others massage the numbers to soften the pain. In reality most service providers would prefer not to dispatch technicians in the middle of the night or on weekends. It requires setting up on-call procedures and very often generates gripes from technicians who don't like being on call. Service-call coverage is usually linked with response-time considerations. Many companies give priority to clients who have service agreements, especially those who pay in advance for service calls as part of their coverage. There are a number of considerations when estimating and proposing service calls as part of a service agreement.

o Client: How many calls can you expect from this account? Things that need to be considered include the skill level of the staff, the complexity of the system, hours of operation, age of equipment, location, etc. And let's not forget some clients are just pains in the you know what. For whatever reason they never appear satisfied regardless of their irrational demands. I caution offering unlimited service calls to these clients, regardless of the costs added to the estimate. They feel entitled to call out technicians for issues that could be resolved over the phone or the next day. If you do include service calls, especially after hours, you may want to limit the number of calls annually as part of the agreement.

o Hours: Obviously 24/7 coverage can be an expensive addition to a service agreement. Most companies don't have effective methods to estimate this coverage. In reality it's not easy, as there are many variables to consider. I find this coverage to be most effective when it's focused on the specific needs of each client.

The traditional approach is offering service-call coverage during normal business hours: Monday to Friday; 24/7 Monday to Friday; or 24/7/365. In reality the client may only be concerned about weekends or holidays when they don't have a staff member on duty. Why offer 24/7/365 when the client doesn't need it or see the value?

One way or another there will be costs added to the estimate if a client needs to purchase coverage that is perceived as a prerequisite to attaining what they actually want. In today's marketplace clients only want to purchase the services they need. Often their requirements don't align with traditional service offerings. If that's the case with your company, someone needs to raise the issue.

o Response times: There are significant logistics issues when promises are made regarding response times. The location of the facility, technicians, and access are key determining factors. Clarification is also needed regarding verbal, electronic, or onsite response time. I often suggest to my clients they guarantee a one-hour, after-hours response time. Typically they shudder at the thought. Once I clarify I'm speaking about phone response versus onsite, they don't have a problem.

The problem from a service-marketing perspective is the failure to communicate properly the difference between the types of responses. Most companies assume the situation will work itself out once the client is under agreement. Often this is the case, as clients understand they may not see technicians until the following morning rather than in the middle of the night. I think the lost opportunity is not marketing response time more effectively. Beyond service providers that are required by law to provide one-hour, onsite response time, like UL-listed central station alarm providers, most don't sell guaranteed response times. They tend to tread lightly in this area, being more concerned with missing their commitments than marketing their capabilities. The number one reason end users switch service providers is lack of response time. I call that a great marketing opportunity.

• Training: End users of products and systems seek any advantage to control costs. For some, training their staff offers the opportunities to reduce their dependence on service providers. For others, training is needed for in-house staff so they know how to operate the equipment.

Some service providers see end-user training as a bad thing as they fear losing service revenue. Others feel a trained client will help maximize the performance of their product and help reduce the cost of service. It's easy to understand both sides of the situation. One thing I'm sure of: if training is marketed correctly it will drive revenue growth, not decrease it. Informed clients tend to buy more products, which ultimately creates more service opportunities.

A good example of underselling customer training is installers of nurse-call systems. These systems are installed in health-care facilities of all sizes. They are primarily used by medical staff to communicate with patients. Due to nursing staff turnover, periodic training on system operation is needed. Some companies hire trainers with nursing backgrounds to conduct the training. What most of these companies don't do is charge for the training. The common response for why they don't charge is fear these accounts won't pay for something they've been receiving at no charge. My first recommendation is to make the training more visible on their service agreements. Overview the training, the number of sessions, and the nursing staff shifts that will receive it as part of the service agreement. If it's presented in this fashion, it will help highlight the value they are providing. Even if they don't charge the customer, they're demonstrating the value in a service-agreement relationship.

Training isn't the easiest offering to justify in a service agreement. Some progressive service providers actually promote it as a way to reduce the cost of a service agreement. They feel if the in-house staff is trained, they are less likely to call for issues that could be solved without the help of the service provider.

- Other services: Beyond the items listed above, there are numerous other offerings that could be bundled into a service agreement. It all depends on the product and equipment that needs to be serviced and the ability of the service provider to deliver the services. Other services may include:

  o Critical parts stocking.
  o Telephone and electronic tech support.
  o Documentation—customized reports.
  o Equipment trade-in, rental, or loaners.
  o Remote monitoring.
  o System upgrade programs.
  o Subcontracted services—single-source solutions.

Service Agreement

A well-crafted service offering requires a well-crafted service agreement. Many companies take pride in presenting great service proposals supported by some great sales aids, but this is more likely the exception than the rule.

Salespeople expend considerable time prospecting for clients, making sales calls, conducting surveys, estimating costs, and creating service offerings that meet their clients' needs. Unfortunately it can all fall apart when it is formatted into a poorly designed service agreement. More often than not, service agreements are not user friendly. They don't highlight the benefits of the services proposed. Most are terms-and-conditions heavy and information light. In short most look like crap. It's often hard to distinguish them from packing lists. Some are pieced together from other companies. They are disjointed and often incoherent. Many are black and white—literally. Little effort is made to coordinate branding with the company's look and feel. Logos are misplaced, unnecessary taglines take up too much space, and there is little appreciation for white space as information is jammed in to minimize pages.

Beyond the services being provided, the service agreement is part of the offering. It not only displays what is being offered; it also presents the company. If it looks unprofessional and dated, that's the impression the client will come away with. Not only will the client review the agreement but he will most likely pass it to one or more people in his purchasing, legal, operations, or management staff. The most frustrating fact is it's only paper. We're talking pennies if a hard copy is used and nothing if it's sent electronically. Most of my clients had used the same service agreements for years. In some cases it was just an oversight. In other situations there was no one on staff who had the skills or time to improve it.

A commonly mentioned barrier when looking to upgrade a service agreement is the need to get input from multiple people, including the much feared legal department. Whatever the excuse don't overlook the importance of a professionally packaged and branded service agreement. A good service agreement should have a template that allows for easy assembly and combines both standardization and room for customization. It shouldn't look like an extended warranty or something manufactured by a service-agreement cookie-cutter machine. It's the exhaust of the service salesperson's efforts.

The client deserves the best you have to offer. The service agreement is a tangible representation of your company's capabilities. I don't even know what your service agreement looks like, but I'm certain I can improve it.

Chapter 8

PRICING
DON'T DISCOUNT ITS IMPORTANCE

You've got a hot prospect. He's been properly qualified and you're confident the WFAN criteria have been satisfied. As you drive away, reality starts to set in: he can't afford to purchase your services. You start to mull over creative solutions. The prospect clearly stated what services he was interested in. You have nothing to offer that meets his needs based on available funding. The initial feeling is frustration, but it quickly turns to disappointment.

For some the next stage is anger directed at their employers for setting such high prices. The only thing that stands between a sale and a nice incentive check is the price of the services. *How do they expect me to sell anything with the prices we're charging? Who set these prices? Have they ever tried to sell a service agreement? Don't they understand how tough competition is?* You're a victim. You feel sorry for yourself and plan on making your feelings known when you return to your office or the laptop that serves as your office.

My advice, get over it! Every good salesperson expects to close every proposal. Good salespeople believe they can sell where no man or woman has sold before. Some are driven by ego or supreme confidence in their abilities. But in the real sales world even the best of us need large doses of humility to succeed. Salespeople have to deal with failure—lots of failure. Other jobs also have to deal with it, but there are few where failure is experienced at such a high rate. It goes beyond not getting the order. It's apparent every time you can't connect with a prospect or decision maker you so desperately want to engage. It surfaces when what you promised a customer falls short of the service actually delivered, and they complain. It hurts when a prospect cancels an appointment on short notice, even when he promises to reschedule.

Sometimes failure is subtle, like when your manager jokes you're only 95 percent of your sales plan. Sometimes it's not so subtle, like when a customer tells you your price is too high and she's decided to go with someone else. If you're in a service sales position and close over 50 percent of your proposals, consider yourself fortunate. Let's be honest: if you close everything you propose you're either not pursuing enough business, picking the cherries that drop in your lap, or working for a company that is mismanaged. If every one of your prospects purchases what you're offering and doesn't squawk about the price you're either working in organized crime or your company is under pricing its services. Anyone, including a trained chimpanzee, could deliver a proposal and get an order if selling service were that easy.

Selling didn't come easily to me. I had been exposed to selling early, as my father had been in men's clothing sales. I worked with him starting in the seventh grade. I would go to his store after school every day, on Saturday's, and in the summer. For the most part I was doing the monotonous stuff like refolding shirts, including the perfect replacement of every pin and insert. Within a short time, I was waiting on customers and doing what I came to realize was selling.

One thing I noticed whenever someone questioned my father about the price of an item he would point out a feature, like permanent-press material or all-leather soles, or remind the customer he was buying a good brand. He rarely offered discounts. I know when he did he felt bad about it. I could see it in the way his demeanor changed and in his shortness when he ordered me to restock merchandise.

Another person who worked with us would always resort to reducing the price by 10 percent. I liked my dad's approach and perceived the other guy as weak. I hated being called a salesman. I'm not sure if I actually hated the job or if I didn't like working with my father and the constant scrutiny that came with it. Selling was not on any short or long list of possible career choices. Salesmen were manipulative people who always seemed to be smiling and had some need to shake hands with friends and strangers, including sheepish, young kids like me.

My negative attitude toward salesman was primarily based on observing my father's haggling over prices on just about everything he bought. It was a complete contradiction in that he sold and purchased differently. He sold performance but bought price. This was in a time when it seemed every store in our area operated in a "hey buddy, I'm a friend of (fill in the blank), so give me a special deal" kind of world. It didn't matter if we were buying another used car or getting our lawn mower repaired. There was always a deal "because I know you." It turned me off. I thought it was dishonest and embarrassing behavior. It was pretty clear there was no deal, but it made the buyer seem special. Observing these deal-making dramas may be the reason why I'm a sell-performance and not a price kind of guy.

After college I was intent on going to law school, but things changed the summer before I enrolled. I was working as a bellhop/busboy/bartender/waiter/night-desk clerk/phone operator in a New York Catskill Mountains hotel. I was making some serious money via tips and was living the tax-free life. I had a great group of peers who were in the same places in their lives as I was. It was at this point where I realized what interested me most was observing people's behavior. As a service provider in my various jobs I interacted with all types of individuals in a multitude of circumstances. I also realized the sales offered me an opportunity to explore my interest.

I decided I didn't want to go to law school. I wanted to take a break after graduation and go off on my own, to make some money and figure out my next step in a year or so. The hardest part was breaking the news to my number one fan, my mom. She always wanted the best for me, and an education was my ticket to a better life. As usual I had underestimated her. She handled it well.

"You know what you're doing. I trust you." Those were her exact words. That's one super mom. No way in hell would I ever let her down.

Now back to the subject at hand: price. It's the bane of many a service salesperson's existence. Overcoming the price issue is part of every salesperson's job. Their companies provide services and need to make profits to pay technicians and service salespeople, satisfy stakeholders, etc. At the same time, clients want to spend as little as possible so their companies can make more profits. Rarely do both parties walk away completely satisfied.

I've made sales calls with hundreds of different salespeople. I'm fairly certain the price issue came up in conversation, in one form or another, every time. Sometimes it was as subtle as the savvy person who would suggest we could grow our business if we could slightly adjust our price points. The more confident ones would reference competition or lost orders. The hot shots would pledge to sell even more if they had some "flexibility" with pricing. I'd patiently listen, pretend to understand, and conclude the conversation by offering a big-picture explanation. I would explain the costs associated with running the service operation and the overall impact service revenue had on the company, and remind them of their generous compensation plans. Most just needed to be heard and felt better, I think, after our conversations. I'm sure they told their spouses and friends they offered up a great suggestion that opened my eyes.

It's true my eyes were opened. They opened to a page where I made a note that this particular individual would receive special scrutiny if his name should pass my way for a promotion. Of course I'm exaggerating a bit, but in all honesty I never felt price was the issue in any of my positions. Somewhere early on I decided selling service was about performance, not price. This statement is the foundation of my sales beliefs.

There are two ways to interpret the statement "sell performance, not price." The typical translation would suggest salespeople focus on the service and performance of their companies. The conversation would convey how price should not be the client's major concern. The main concern should be properly maintaining equipment by receiving quality service.

I have another twist on this statement that is more personal. I felt, and still feel, my personal performance in the sales call is equally important to my company's performance. If I can't make a client understand what I'm offering is of value, regardless of the cost, I have failed. I don't think I'm driven by my oversized ego but a sense of taking responsibility for my own actions. I've never been prone to making excuses. I almost always accept a bad sales call didn't go my way and move on. I did say *almost* always. There have been many occasions when I wanted to give the prospect a high five to the head. By the way the "move on" part is very important. Salespeople need to clear their heads of negative feelings for the next call.

Typically price occupies a big piece of mindshare with sales representatives. Most good salespeople learn to deal with it by perfecting their prospecting and qualifying skills. They seek prospects in market segments more receptive to a well-crafted value propositions. The good ones have also honed their qualifying skills by enlightening their prospects about what it takes to maintain their equipment and why their company is the best choice.

Unfortunately for many salespeople, the price issue becomes the major barrier to finding success. They just can't get over it. Even in interviews with prospective hires, price works its way into the conversation when weak candidates speak of past employers. Typically it applies to all of their past employers. It's normally a package deal—"our service wasn't that great" and "we charged more than our competition." These individuals perceive themselves as victims of an unjust situation.

I believe these price-conscious individuals, once addicted, never alter their thoughts or behavior. They wake up as price-obsessed junkies and remain that way throughout the day. They meet with clients and believe they are at a disadvantage before any words are spoken. Some try to oversell their companies' capabilities and sound like used-car salesmen. Some immediately go into defensive modes and only present their lowest levels of service offerings. Others may speak poorly about competition. The worst offenders apologize to their prospects for having to charge them so much and blame their situations on their employers. That last example is inexcusable and cowardly behavior even when it results in getting orders.

Why are so many service salespeople price sensitive? Based on my experience, there are a number of reasons.

- Poor training. When salespeople lack the necessary skills to qualify prospects they go into sales calls unprepared. They lack the proper service-sales training so they resort to unprofessional methods. Typically, weak communication techniques limit their abilities to develop calls in a way that focuses on the prospect's situation rather than their own shortcomings. They stumble through calls spending too much time rapport-building and trying to make friends with clients. Their lack of skills puts them in situations where price becomes the driving force in the calls.

Highly trained, professional salespeople know price is a reality, but it doesn't become a barrier to their performances. They don't feel they're victims of a bad economy, the market environment, or company policies. They don't let competition set the standard. They believe they are in control of most outcomes.

- Too much information. Many companies that market service still utilize estimating formats based on time and material formulas. They price labor, materials, and other associated costs and simply add them together. Most will add a markup.

For the most part this is a time and material-pricing strategy for a service agreement. Not only does this method of estimating service agreements fall short of best practices, but it exposes too much information to the salesperson. They will make value judgments based on specific costs, including labor rates, gross margin targets, and gross profits. Everything is transparent, leaving too much room for interpretation. This is like crack for analytical salespeople. They cut estimates into pieces, partition off the good and bad, and hit the street feeling they've scored. In essence they have become their own dealers.

The price of a service agreement should not equal the sum of the parts. It's very common for a client to ask for a breakout of the pricing for various inclusions in a service agreement. If that's easily done, I suggest changes need to be made. A service agreement is not a time and material job relabeled as a service agreement. It's a package of services that typically includes both hard and soft deliverables that benefit the client. In most cases the cost of the whole should actually be more than the sum of the parts.

- Wrong career. People find themselves in sales careers for a number of reasons. At the top of the list is the fact that there are a large number of sales positions available. Most don't require any unique knowledge or education. I think most of us just fell into sales positions, realized it was a pretty good situation, and made careers out of it. At the same time others fell into sales jobs and probably should have held out for something else. They don't have the communication skills, abstract thinking ability, or people skills necessary to succeed. They plod along somewhere slightly below or above average. As Sheryl Crow once sang, "If it makes you happy it can't be that bad." So who am I to judge?

    Based on my experience the reasons why people choose sales as a career fall into three groups: "I like people, so sales was perfect for me"; "I couldn't sit at a desk all day. I need to be out and about". "The money is good, and I've never missed any of my kid's baseball games." Personally I think the third rationale is the best. It has a good balance of work and family and an implied understanding that being successful at selling will earn you some freedom.

- "You can't handle the truth." Jack Nicolson's memorable line in *A Few Good Men* sums it up. Service revenue is critical to the financial performance of all companies. For some it's the lifeblood that keeps the doors open and pays the rent. For manufacturers it provides the revenue needed for the research and development of new products. For companies large and small it's needed to cover the lost profits from no, or low-margin product and system sales.

Service revenue keeps technicians employed during soft economic times and helps companies level out swings in cash flow. Companies take service revenue into account when forecasting cash needs and when applying for financing from their banks. Service is very profitable if marketed correctly. It shouldn't be compared to the profit generated by sales of products or systems. It's in its own class of business. Do some companies overcharge? Yes. Do some charge excessively and take advantage of their customers? Yes. The truth be told, service has profit and margin expectations that may seem excessive to some salespeople. What they don't understand is how it fits into the overall business models of their companies. In most cases it's not an important part of the business—it's the business.

Even though estimating follows surveying in the sales cycle, it actually comes into play earlier. Service salespeople know the basic costs of their services and work hard to ascertain their prospects' needs relative to the funding available. As the conversation develops, a good salesperson is already mentally quantifying what he will be in a position to offer during the first call. He is qualifying and estimating simultaneously. He begins to frame the offering and position it with the prospect during the qualifying call.

Unfortunately for many salespeople and companies, this can be the point where the potential sale begins to break down. A major barrier to service sales success is what I call the *authorization hurdle*. Due to the lack of a good estimating system or confidence in their sales staff, companies put approval procedures in place. If the salesperson offers anything beyond the norm he must have his estimate approved by one or multiple people. It's a time-consuming and frustrating exercise that more often than not will cause the salesperson not to propose the best solution. He may even hear the prospect verbalize her specific needs but lead her in another direction. He visualizes the hassle of getting the estimate approved and doesn't want to make the effort or get shot down. In almost all cases these approval hurdles are unnecessary if a well-conceived service-sales program is in place.

I was recently hired by a large company that was seeking help to grow their service business. They are a market leader and manufacture a product that is the best in its class. Their market share is approximately 40 percent and their brand is well respected. The current economic situation slowed their product sales, as it did with many other companies, and they are looking to service as a solution.

As part of my research I asked to speak with a representative group of their sales personnel across the country. I interviewed about a dozen individuals who sold both products and service. Every salesperson liked the company, and most had worked there for multiple years. I was surprised they all acknowledged they had a good service department, which is not typically the case when discussing service with salespeople.

They had good sales aids and customers were receptive to their service offerings, but sales were flat. The primary obstacle was the company and its structure. All service agreements that included multi-location accounts needed to be approved by service and sales management. This was a common situation, as the company's primary market included national chain stores. Salespeople would prepare estimates and forward them to the appropriate parties. The process could take anywhere from three days to three weeks.

In almost every case they would get approved. After gaining my assurance that I would not single her out to management, one person summed up the problem: "It's a hassle to sell service. It's not worth my time." All this company needed to do was to improve their estimating format and eliminate the unnecessary bureaucracy they had in place. In reality almost everyone knew it was a problem, but no one did anything about it. As in most firms I work with, everyone was too busy doing other things to focus on service marketing.

Pricing can come into play even earlier. Most overachieving service salespeople target prospects who are less likely to be price sensitive. A good example would be people who have the option of selling service to both the private and public sectors. In almost all cases there is more room for negotiation when selling to the private sector. The public sector is often bound by rules for bidder qualification that can attract competition normally not found in the negotiated world of the private sector. Typically services are competitively bid and generic, and accountability for work performed is minimal. So why would a person selling service target the public sector when there are private sector opportunities available? The good ones don't!

The degree of flexibility service salespeople have when pricing service agreements varies widely. For many, price levels are predetermined by their companies and selected off a price list. Some are generated by an estimating system with little or no room for adaptation. For others there is a great deal of flexibility in the customization and pricing of service offerings. These individuals have the ability to configure offerings that not only provide more value for their clients but also generate more profits for their employers. A good example would be agreements that include no-charge service call coverage. Let's assume you're selling a service agreement that only includes inspecting or testing a product. There's some obvious risk when including service calls. If that same client purchased an agreement that included preventive maintenance, the likelihood of unplanned service calls would be reduced. By including maintenance the agreement may warrant less labor cost to cover service calls. The incremental additional cost of the agreement may provide a huge gain in value for the client.

Another example that may require overriding established pricing guidelines would be strategic accounts. *Strategic* may mean an account that buys a great deal of product or may be planning a major purchase in the future. In some situations strategic means taking business from a competitor to gain access to a new customer or defending an attack by a competitor on a current client. Whatever the reason there are situations that may require special treatment. They should be the exceptions, not the norm. Tagging accounts as strategic is often just a mechanism to justify discounting service. If a service salesperson's strategy is discounting, then I guess it would be strategic in his eyes. In mine, it's just poor salesmanship.

In summary the cost of the services you sell may be a harsh reality, but it is reality. Good people need to look past this issue and not wait for the situation to change. Yes there are companies that price service like a commodity and leave little room for negotiation by well-intended salespeople. In all honesty these situations shouldn't occur, but they do. If you work for one of these companies, pass on my contact information. I'd be more than willing to help improve your situation.

Chapter 9

PROPOSAL
WILL YOU BE MINE?

The proposal is the documented presentation that demonstrates the effort, thoroughness, and professionalism of a service salesperson. It's the written description of the services to be performed. The proposal is the final analysis of the survey and the end product of the estimating process. Most important it's the right solution for the client based on information obtained during the qualification process.

The proposal is the intersection of objective information from conversations and observations and the step in the sales cycle where subjectivity comes into play. At this point in the sales cycle, the time for analyzing and posturing is over. It's time to pull everything together and prepare the proposal for the prospect. For some it's the point where they realize they're missing some important information and will revisit the client and/or site. Others may choose to create the proposal though they're lacking information and must do some guessing. It's not too late to reconfirm a missing billing address, part number, or start date. These types of clerical oversights are not unusual and can be resolved with a phone call or e-mail.

On the other hand if the salesperson is at a loss regarding whose name should be placed in the signature area, the available funding, or what services are needed, that's a problem—a big problem. If this is the case, a proposal should not be prepared. A proposal prepared with insufficient information typically produces an unsatisfactory result for both the client and the salesperson.

Many salespeople admit creating and finalizing proposals is their biggest stumbling block. Procrastination is common as some salespeople postpone the task as long as possible. For some it's the realization they haven't properly qualified the prospect. They know they're in weak positions to prepare the proposals confidently. Feelings of anxiety are not unusual as salespeople realize at this point in the sales cycle they need to make some tough decisions.

For many it's the mechanics and time needed to construct a proposal that puts them off. I also find many salespeople procrastinate because they're too busy prospecting and making sales calls. For some reason they think preparing proposals for already qualified prospects doesn't take priority over looking for new business. It must be some kind of "counting your chickens before the eggs hatched" complex.

Every salesperson has skills that come naturally. Many enjoy the hunt and are expert prospectors. Some excel in the investigative nature of the qualification process. Few enjoy creating proposals. Most salespeople don't like to interrupt their daily routines and do this type of work. Many perceive it as administrative grunt work. Overachieving service salespeople understand the sooner they prepare the proposals the sooner they can present them to their clients. They know as time passes key information and a sense for the client and their needs may diminish. They also know if they wait longer than needed to prepare and present the proposal, the client may lose interest and momentum. This doesn't imply every proposal should be presented as quickly as possible. It implies the proposal should be prepared as soon as possible to ensure the quality of the information. I will cover when to present the proposal in the next chapter.

By definition a proposal is something presented to someone for consideration. It's a common term in the business, legal, entertainment, and writing professions. It should be packaged to present something to someone in the best way possible. Proposals are made to entice people to do things. In the case of service marketing, we're trying to entice prospects to purchase the services we are offering.

Obviously the salesperson also plays a large role in motivating the prospect to buy. Some companies overemphasize the role of the salesperson and underestimate the importance of the proposal. Other companies put emphasis on submitting proposals to prospects without any support from a salesperson. They craft beautiful proposals they believe will sell themselves. This may be the case, but clearly the best chance for success is a well-trained services salesperson armed with a great proposal.

I received a call from a client I'm working with in Florida. I'm currently putting together her service sales aids with the intention of launching her program after she hires a dedicated services salesperson. My client mentioned she was calling on a prospect and was able to see a proposal from another firm competing for the business. She asked me if that company was a client of mine. As they were listed on my Website, I acknowledged they were.

Her response: "I knew they must be. The proposal was beautiful. I assumed it was yours." She actually used the word "beautiful." Needless to say I was flattered. She said by comparison hers was embarrassing and she couldn't wait to receive the new one I'm developing for her company.

There's no reason a proposal should be anything less than beautiful. It should contain great information but also provide some eye candy for the prospect. A well-designed proposal is the most important sales aid a person has available when it comes to selling service. In almost all cases, it's the only thing a prospect can see and feel when contemplating purchasing a service agreement.

For the most part a proposal, when selling service, is the service agreement. The proposal and the agreement are usually one and the same. As you may have already noticed, at this point in the book I use the term *agreement*, not *contract*. Some believe the words are synonyms. I don't. An agreement denotes parties, seller and buyer, agreeing on something. In the service world it imparts to the client the service provider has agreed to provide the services outlined and the customer agrees to pay for them. Agreement implies a partnership has been created between the parties and they will make their best efforts to comply. In reality an agreement is also a legal document, but there is value in semantics.

As for the word *contract*, it is what it is. It's a legal document both parties will sign and enter into. I know, from research done in this area, prospects perceive the word *agreement* more positively than *contract*. I know when a proposal is presented as a *service agreement* it generates a more positive response than when a *service contract* is proposed. *Contract* is a harsh, legal term that often creates an adversarial relationship on its own. There is far greater advantage in proposing services that are presented in an agreement format than in dropping a service contract in front of a prospect. Clients are more apt to value solutions presented in an agreement than tasks presented in a contract. The packaging of a proposal should not be overlooked. For many prospects the service offering/proposal is the product you are selling.

I often refer to the creation of proposals as *crafting*. I use the term as one would use *craft* to describe a special skill. I believe the development of a great proposal is a special skill. Some salespeople will add special provisions to agreements that are sure to impress prospects. They could be as simple as putting the contact information of users of the equipment or the name of the individual who should be contacted to schedule a service call. I've seen agreements that include special provisions such as where the service vehicle should park and a call chain should an emergency arise, and even a provision that requested service personnel didn't fraternize with the client's employees.

Some service salespeople focus on composing great cover letters or including technical information or news-related items that may support their proposals. These tactics can even be utilized by salespeople who have little ability to alter anything in their companies' service agreements. In lieu of customizing the agreement, they personalize the sales aids submitted with it. When it comes to crafting a proposal, anything that sets yours apart from your competition's or supports your value proposition should be considered. There's always room for creativity.

The proposal is also a place where a person selling service can impart market knowledge. A good example would be including references to codes or regulations that directly affect the client. The salesperson can include exact copies of regulatory documentation or specific statements that support the purchase of the service agreement. What may be more effective is reminding the client that by purchasing the service agreement the uptime of their equipment will improve, disruption of employees will be minimized, or their specific workload will be reduced. The last point is an area of particular importance for many decision makers. Many have been confronted with budget cuts and manpower reductions that probably have them working more hours or expanding their responsibilities. A well-crafted proposal should not only overview the services but also demonstrate how it fits into the overall business strategy of the client.

Other Considerations
- Service purchasing history.
- In-house staff capabilities.

- The client's personal views and values.
- The corporate culture.
- Current and previous service providers.
- Fiscal year versus calendar year.

Normally the topic of a lack of confidence arises when discussing an underperforming service salesperson's ability to qualify prospects or close sales. I find it also applies to proposal preparation. I'm constantly reassuring new and experienced salespeople they're experts at what they do. Far too many underestimate their experience and knowledge. I remind them they are probably some of the most experienced people selling service in their areas because they do it every day. Regardless of the product they need to accept the fact they are experts at selling service. Even new service salespeople, especially those dedicated to only selling service, become experts in a few months.

This confidence needs to surface when preparing a proposal. A salesperson gains confidence with every sale. They also gain confidence from knowing the proposals they're presenting are impressive in both content and appearance. Clients can sense when salespeople aren't confident in what they are proposing. It raises the specter of doubt in their minds. This doesn't infer the salespeople should be so sure of themselves they come across as arrogant or cocky. Neither of those attitudes works well in sales. I'm speaking about the confidence projected by someone who knows what she's doing. It's the assurance and confidence one would gain from a trusted advisor. People rarely buy from people they don't trust. I know I don't.

The concept of being the expert and trusted advisor comes apparent when discussing the subject of offering service options to clients. By *options* I mean submitting multiple proposals to the same client. It can also mean the choice of options within one proposal. In one case it's separate documents; in the other it's check boxes.

In either case I'm not a big supporter of the multi-choice service-marketing strategy. I believe it undermines the whole sales process. It's like admitting to the client, "I don't know what you need or want, so pick what you like." WFAN becomes WFA? The salesperson is no longer a trusted advisor but a proposal preparer. He becomes a commodity trader rather than a professional salesperson. The qualifying call becomes generic as the salesperson primarily needs to determine the decision-making process and information regarding the equipment. Who cares about funding if you're going to bring back a menu of services? Why show artificial concern for their needs when you're just going to generate a generic proposal?

I'm not speaking about companies that offer multiple levels of service like gold, silver, or bronze. I'm speaking about a sales strategy where multiple levels of service are offered in a proposal format for clients to choose. Typically they review the various options and try to place values on the differences between them. Based on my studies on this subject, they most commonly pick the one in the middle, if they pick one at all.

I know there are counter arguments to my position. You probably will have a couple of them before you finish this paragraph. Trust me, I've heard them all multiple times. They range from "the customer is always right" to "I think it's easier for the client to understand what we have to offer." If this book were about selling products, my opinion may be different, but it's about selling service. Marketing service isn't as simple as comparing the features and benefits of products. There's some consistency in product specifications and features. In the case of service, the product's age, application, and usage rule the day. It requires crafting and offering a unique proposal for each client's specific needs. I would rather prepare and submit another proposal than present a proposal with a menu of choices. By the way most overachieving service salespeople don't often find themselves in situations that call for submitting another proposal. Of course they know how to qualify their prospects and craft great proposals.

As mentioned earlier some service agreements/proposals just look bad. Many look like random pieces of information scattered across paper. It's not unusual to see multiple type sizes or fonts, or misspelled words. I'm sure somewhere in this book there are misspelled words even after using spell check countless times and having the copy reviewed by an editor. I'm also certain there are problems with my grammar and syntax. Was that my intent? No. This is a book, not a service agreement. It contains tens of thousands of words. A service agreement should be a perfect, well-developed template. It's a direct reflection on the quality of the salesperson and the company he represents.

Many of my clients think their agreements are just fine until I start to point out issues. They believe they're sufficient, but sufficient isn't good enough. In truth most companies haven't taken hard looks at their agreements in years. That's why most are outdated, and find their way to the "I'll get to it later" pile for many clients.

A good proposal needs to engage the client. When he first views it he will quickly decide if he should take the time to read it. The volume and content of what we read has seen phenomenal changes over recent years. Numerous studies have shown our attention spans have been reduced. A service proposal needs to be designed for today's audience, not yesterdays.

Another criterion for an effective service agreement is a good template. It should be easy to use. For example I developed a template for one of my primary markets that is thirty pages. The key word is *template*. The average service agreement for this market is about six to eight pages. Within the template are all of the service offerings a salesperson may need to propose. The salesperson can also select from three pages of potential special provisions common to this market. The template is constructed in a way that anyone with cut-and-paste skills can create a great proposal in less than ten minutes. It makes it easy for users to select and alter any offering. They can also add their own special provisions over time. What they have is a living document that can be adapted to any customer or situation. What was once a chore is now a simple procedure that improves productivity.

A lot of information transpires during a good sales call. Prospects convey important information that needs to be considered when preparing the proposal. Some of it's clear in meaning and content. Other information is subtle. Good salespeople take notes. They jot down key information without disrupting the pace of the call. It demonstrates interest to the prospect and helps the salesperson recall needed information at a later time.

Unfortunately some of the best information doesn't always make its way into the proposal. Typically it's simply a lack of a place to insert it. If the proposal is of the cookie-cutter variety the only way to document additional information may be in an e-mail or a letter. Any correspondence needs to be short and sweet in today's business world, so it may limit what needs to be said. If multiple items or a short paragraph are required they are either lost in translation or ignored.

Another problem with letters and e-mails is they don't always travel with the proposal. The prospect may forward the proposal to someone in her organization without the correspondence attached. Important information that supports the proposal is lost, which may result in a lost sale.

Presentable

Everyone has been prompted by a parent or seen it happen in a movie: "Make yourself presentable" as they straighten a young person's tie or comb their hair. This is also the case with a good service proposal. It has to be presentable. It has to present itself well, but I'm not speaking about good looks. I'm referring to presenting the proposal to the client face to face. Some salespeople refer to this as walking the client through the proposal. I think this description fits.

The proposal is like a story. It has a beginning, middle, and end. It begins with an overview of the services provided. Then it describes the actual tasks to be performed. It ends with a call to action, a place to sign. A one or two-page proposal with an additional page of terms and conditions is not presentable. You hand it to the client and it just stares back at him. He sees some names and addresses and a price. He scans a few lines or check boxes describing the services and then looks blankly at you. Yep, there it is: a service agreement. The client sees his company's name and address, and a price. That's pretty much it. Have a nice day.

As a salesperson you then go into sell mode and share more information with the client. This is hard work. Selling a piece of paper isn't easy, especially if you're asking thousands of dollars for it. Trying to get $6,000 for a line on a page that says "one annual test and inspection" is a major challenge. Trying to sell a line that reads, "parts included" for $9,000 is just plain scary.

A good service proposal should be presentable. There should be informative and enlightening information in it that can be reviewed with the client. It may include a list of detailed information about the maintenance procedures to be performed or the benefits of the service. As mentioned really good proposals have areas to incorporate special provisions that apply specifically to the client. No one likes to read boilerplate information. A good service proposal actually has more than a beginning, middle, and end. It should include who, what, how, and why and end with the client understanding how it's the solution to his needs.

Keys to a Presentable Proposal

- **Customer oriented:** Think in terms of what the prospect perceives as her needs. It may differ from what was determined by the salesperson or the company's traditional positioning of service offerings. In most cases they are similar, but they need to be positioned in the proposal with the prospect in mind. Sometimes it's only a matter of shifting the emphasis in certain areas in the proposal. That can be accomplished by highlighting the client's concerns in the documentation or verbally. A standard service agreement or canned sales presentation is typically not customer oriented.

- **Benefits and solutions:** People purchase benefits and solutions, not products and services. Most people selling service speak in terms of benefits and solutions during the sales call but present the client with service offerings and fail to focus on their benefits. This shouldn't be the case. Obviously an overview of the services to be provided is needed, but each service offering should have an explanation of the benefits to be received. This is often where information gets eliminated or condensed when misguided service providers are too focused on quantity and not the quality of their service proposals.

- **Simple language:** Services shouldn't be described in technical jargon. All too often the use of acronyms and tech speak is prevalent in service proposals. Some of the terms are the results of labels firms add to their services, like *preferred, premium,* or *select.* Another major issue is acronyms associated with the service industry by regulatory agencies like NFPA, OSHA, UL, etc. Most disconcerting are the technical terms used to describe services that clients may not understand. Terms like *sensitivity testing, calibration, hydrostatic testing,* or even a simple term like *balancing* that is used in HVAC services come to mind.

- **Provides answers:** Many years ago talk-show host Johnny Carson portrayed a character called Carnac the Magnificent. A turban wearing psychic, Carnac would hold a sealed envelope containing a question to his brow. He would predict the answer before opening the envelope. A good service proposal should the same. It should contain the answer to every potential question the prospect may ask. Typically the questions become predicable over time. There is no reason the majority of them can't be addressed in the proposal.

- **Stand on its own:** Many service proposals are sold without face-to-face presentations. Even when presented in person they may be sent to other people in the client's company for review. A good service proposal should be able to present itself. It needs to be understood by individuals who have little knowledge regarding the products to be serviced. It's fairly easy to see if your current proposal can pass the test. Pass it along to your significant other, or, even better, a teenager, and see if it makes sense to them.

- **Complete:** Mundane information can't be overlooked. Billing addresses, start dates, contact information, etc. all need to be accurate. If this information is correct and the services proposed are explained in detail, the client should approve the proposal. Many clients use the smallest oversights to prolong their purchases. Don't give them the opportunity to procrastinate at your expense.

One of the most common topics when reviewing my clients' current service agreements is length. How many pages should an agreement be? Normally my response is not in line with the client's opinion. Usually a debate ensues among my colleagues, and the same discussion points come up every time:

"Clients won't read all of this information!"

"Anything more than two pages is too much!"

"We need to have a proposal our salespeople can present on the spot, so one page is all we can use."

"A lot of pages will intimidate the client."

"Too much information begs for questions."

After they've made their cases I ask them to tell me how they know what they're saying is correct. What type of research have they done with their clients to confirm these views? As expected, it's limited, to say the least. Normally it's the opinions of a couple of people in the office or a comment from a client or two. My sense is most of the justifications for oversimplified proposals are due to either the laziness or the lack of creativity of the sales and administrative people who have to prepare them. The most common offending group is service operations. They voice their concerns that they will not be able to manage service agreements that are not standardized. They almost always acknowledge this may be what customers want, but that's beside the point. That statement speaks for itself. In almost all cases, the reasons for limiting the length of the proposal are internal issues. They're company oriented, not customer oriented. That's just wrong.

The length of the proposal should be self-determining. It shouldn't be filled with information that meets a page count criteria. It's not about the page count. It's about presenting the information discussed over the course of this chapter.

Sometimes the problem is obvious when I see proposal pages filled from top to bottom. This isn't a coincidence. They look like they were prepared by an engineer who was given the task of fitting everything into the square inches available. If extra space were required, they chose to eliminate information rather than add another page. They couldn't allow any white space. A half-filled page is unspeakable.

The creation of a proposal template should start with outlining all of the information that needs to be communicated. Strong consideration needs to be given to presenting information in a way that is understood by the client and others who may be reviewing the agreement. A good proposal is, ironically, like many television comedies. They seem to be written to please everyone. Some would say they are written to appeal to the lowest common denominator of their target audiences. In short, they are dumbed down.

A service proposal should not be written so only the informed buyer understands it. This is very typical in the technical-services industry. It's the primary reason why tech speak and bad graphics are found in many service providers' sales aids. When content is finalized, the layout and graphic treatment should be done by someone with experience in design, not someone from operations. Once it's completed it doesn't hurt to present it to a cross section of clients to gain some feedback. As mentioned, for many clients the service agreement/proposal is the product. It's not just some paper with stuff on it. It shouldn't look like an edict you see nailed to a door in movies set in previous centuries. The proposal should be considered an integral part of a service provider's sales and marketing strategy. It's very, very, very important.

Chapter 10

PRESENTATION
IN SEARCH OF A STANDING OVATION

A proposal can be delivered and presented in various ways. The traditional, face-to-face sales meeting is usually the desired method, but it isn't always feasible. The client can also be presented with a proposal electronically, by mail, by phone, or through a combination of all three. Regardless of the communication method, the presentation is the step in the sales cycle when the prospect receives a proposal to review. Important when selecting the mode of delivery is the need to attract the correct level of attention for the proposal. Without question, great presentations impact close rates.

In some cases a great presentation can enhance a mediocre proposal and persuade a client to make a purchase. If this weren't the case, the Home Shopping Network or QVC may not exist and countless jewelry items and cooking aids never would have been created for people to spend their hard-earned money on. A more relevant example is the restaurant business. The term *presentation* is often used to describe how food is delivered and displayed for the customer. When it comes to marketing service agreements on technology-based products and systems, the presentation of the services being proposed is an important step in the sales cycle.

Plain and simple the primary goal of the presentation is getting the order. Style and substance are important, but in the end receiving approval for the proposal is what matters most.

The only true measurement of presentation success is getting the order. It's not about receiving compliments, accolades, or heartwarming thanks from clients. I've given presentations that were so good I had to talk myself out of quitting sales and moving to New York to share my talents with Broadway audiences. On a few occasions I became distracted by my own superior presentations skills and lost track of where I was. I recall a few times when I cut off clients from speaking as I was in the midst of delivering great orations that had to continue without interruption.

These were all great demonstrations of my prowess as a master of the presentation and my bloated ego. If I think hard, reluctantly, there were probably a few duds. In all seriousness, what I thought about my performances was irrelevant. The only thing that mattered was getting or not getting the order. I've made many sales after delivering great presentations and when I really sucked. One thing I'm fairly certain of is I never lost a sale because I made a great presentation. I know I lost deals because I did a lousy one.

A question I'm commonly asked is: when is the right time to make the presentation? It's usually framed in terms of days after making the first call. Is a week too long or too short? Will I be perceived as overanxious if I tell the prospect I'll get back to him the next day? What if my client declines a meeting and requests I send my presentation electronically ASAP? Is it the best use of my time to travel to a client to make a presentation when I can send it electronically? These are all good questions that don't generate "yes" or "no" answers. Numerous factors come into play.

- **Value:** Size matters in sales. The economics of the situation most often determines the strategy. Big dollar returns usually require big time investments. Traveling a long distance to make a presentation that involves a proposal that will generate a small fraction of your sales goal may not be the best use of time. Delaying a meeting to ensure all the necessary parties are able to attend a key presentation is probably a good idea regardless of the agreement size. A face-to-face presentation is highly recommended when significant dollars are involved.

- **Timing:** Anyone who has sales experience knows momentum can be lost if too much time passes between sales calls. Coordinating the schedules of the client and the people she wants to attend the presentation may create a lengthy delay. Sometimes this situation can't be avoided, but every effort should be made to prevent it. Often the best approach is scheduling the presentation meeting at the conclusion of the qualifying call. It's also another indicator that you have a qualified prospect. It will reveal the prospect's level of interest and sense of urgency. If the prospect indicates she wants to expedite the process that's always a good sign she is prepared to purchase. Take advantage of the situation. A hot prospect shouldn't be left to cool off. If the client has a strong desire to purchase, every effort should be made to get the proposal in front of her as soon as possible.

- **Circumstance:** In some cases unique requests supersede other concerns. People selling service need to provide their services in a timely manner. The prospect may have immediate issues with his equipment. Sending the proposal electronically may be quicker than scheduling a meeting. In some situations the time and cost of a return trip may not be economical. One thing that is consistent when selling service is there is no consistency. Unique situations are the norm. Service salespeople need to be flexible.

- **Offer:** For many salespeople the offer is so straightforward there is little need to make a face-to-face presentation.

This is the case when the proposal is a standardized agreement that requires minimal interpretation. Does a one-page, plain-vanilla service agreement require a high-priced delivery person? Typically little value is added by the service salesperson. As previously mentioned a well-designed service agreement has broad ramifications. Some service proposals, by their own design, require formal presentations to overcome their shortcomings. Properly designed service agreements can often present themselves.

One area that is overlooked by many salespeople is the time and day factor. For many businesspeople the busiest part of the day is first thing in the morning or the end of the day. I think most people's energy and performance diminishes over the day. I know mine does. Some people keep up their pace by drinking coffee, downing energy drinks, or taking snack breaks. Even with the use of stimulants, I think our mental capacities deteriorate later in the day.

For many, early afternoon is used for digesting burritos or responding to e-mails or events that appeared while at lunch. I feel mid-morning is the best time to make a presentation. It allows attendees to get their day started while still having good energy levels before they glide into lunch. I believe the worst time to make a presentation is the end of the day. The clock becomes a factor. The client usually plans on leaving work at a certain time and is preoccupied with that thought. Most people have work that needs to be completed before they depart. Many people have things occurring in their personal lives that require them to leave by certain times.

Time is also a factor for the salesperson. In all honesty I've rushed through four o'clock presentations because I was concerned about beating traffic or missing flights. I'm sure my sense of urgency impacted those meetings in negative ways.

Usually presentations at the end of the day end with indecision. Clients may feel rushed and become too distracted even to ask questions. I also think the day of the week is a factor. I consider Monday and Friday the two volatile days—Monday because it's back-to-work day and things may have piled up over the weekend and Friday because it's Friday.

I think Bob Geldof summed it up for many in his classic tune "I Don't Like Mondays." There are few among us who don't relish Friday afternoon. It's acknowledgement we've survived another week of work and stirs thoughts of that elusive, perfect weekend we dream about. For some it means casual dress or a big lunch with coworkers. For others it's the last chance to make sure their fantasy league is set up for the weekend. For many it's a game of cat and mouse when it comes to how early they can sneak out the door in the afternoon. It's not a good environment for a sales presentation. For these reasons I still schedule Friday as an in-office day. It's also the worst day to travel. I did it as a field salesperson and I do it as a consultant. I do the bulk of my client contact Tuesday through Thursday.

In almost all circumstances, nothing beats a traditional, face-to-face meeting with a client. Most people would rather attend live performances than watch them on TV or read about them. Sure live performances can be inconvenient and expensive, but the elation felt while walking away from a great one can't be experienced sitting behind a desk. I don't care if you have the world's greatest sound system or 3D—it's still not like being there.

The same goes for a sales presentation. Sitting face to face with the client allows you to read her reactions and disposition. It ensures your proposal is being reviewed and positioned in the best way. It also demonstrates your commitment in time and effort. By that I mean the guilt the client hopefully feels in knowing you spent two hours traveling to meet with her. Clients can't see your new haircut or your coordinated purse and shoes in your e-mail. It's hard to comment on how well the client looks over the phone. People like to buy from people, especially in abstract selling environments like service sales. Most of my customer surveys revealed the reason clients chose certain service providers was the people selling the service. Only company reputation was rated higher. That's not to say selling any other way than face to face is undesirable. I'm saying it's the preferred method when it makes economic sense.

Let's review the most common methods for presenting a service proposal.

- **Face to face.** See above. You are a star that needs to be seen!
- **E-mail.** Attaching a PDF of the proposal to a well-crafted e-mail is a viable method for some presentations. Some salespeople will also attach sales aids like PowerPoint presentations or include links to Websites. The obvious shortcoming is confirmation, beyond the e-mail being opened, that the client actually reads the proposal and supporting materials. There are also issues with the formatting of the e-mail and the attached materials. Do you want your information reviewed on a small phone screen? Probably not. It's unrealistic to think a client will give your proposal his undivided attention when it's sent electronically.
- **Mail.** I'm not a big fan of snail mail, but I'm a fan of USPS Priority Mail. I rarely send anything that isn't Priority Mail to my clients. Without question my highest response rates when prospecting are generated by utilizing this method. For example when I use volume e-mails like Constant Contact I have an impressive *open rate* of over thirty percent. When I send prospecting letters to customers via Priority Mail I have a *response rate* of over 25 percent. It's hard for people to ignore a FedEx or Priority Mail

envelope. Even most gatekeepers will pass on mail to their bosses sent with special handling. It may be a bit more expensive, but it's usually worth the small investment.

- **Phone.** Not too long ago using a phone implied having a conversation. Now it also includes e-mails, tweets, and countless applications. Without question a proposal read on a small phone screen isn't going to have the same impact as an 8½ x 11 presentation. The phone is a great sales tool when used correctly. Phone messages are commonly used to follow up on proposals that were sent electronically: "Mr. R. U. Thare, this is Stephen Pitts. I'm calling to follow up on the proposal I sent you. If you have any questions please give me a call." We've all made this call by necessity. It's the reality we live in. As for mobile phones, they're great for social conversations but not very reliable for important business discussions.

- **Combination.** The next best thing to being there is a combination of the above. Forward the proposal and sales aids and schedule a call to review the information. The desired situation is having the client view the information for the first time as you're presenting it over the phone. This requires cooperation from the client to open the information and allow sufficient time to conduct the call. It also requires great presentation skills. The salesperson needs to be concise and have the ability to convey enthusiasm and commitment as well as interpret the client's reaction without visual cues. Obviously this is easier accomplished in person.

All salespeople are unique in their own ways. We all have personalities and styles that are both inherent and learned over time. They surface when making presentations. What works for some may not work for others. I've always considered my ability to make presentations one of my strong points. I'm good, but

I've seen many people who are better. I've watched people make presentations that left me feeling inadequate and depressed. I've watched others look like fools who made me feel like I was part of a bad circus act.

Based on my years of participating in service sales presentations, I find the following styles to be most prevalent. I do favor a certain style, but that's an individual choice every salesperson needs to make. In this case *choice* means keep doing what you're doing if you're successful. If you're not, change!

Consultative

My service sales strategy is consistent with consultative sales techniques. This style has the service salesperson playing the role of consultant. He assists the prospect in identifying her needs and offers solutions. This approach can be utilized in almost all service sales situations as clients typically need enlightenment regarding the service requirements of their equipment.

This presentation style guides the prospect through the proposal in a non-confrontational manner. The service salesperson reviews the needs of the client and then outlines a plan that provides the solution. The communication style is informative and conversational. Most clients are receptive to this approach, but not all. Some personality styles require other approaches to accomplish the goal of getting the order.

Assumptive

The assumptive style is used by confident salespeople who view the presentation as a secondary step in the sales cycle. They assume their skills and expertise will carry the day. They also assume their clients have little choice but to purchase their services, which puts them in the driver's seat.

They present the information in a concise and matter-of-fact way. They allow a few questions and feel offended if clients ask them to prepare additional proposals or alter their offerings. I'm a big fan of confidence in a service salesperson, but that's about all this strategy has to offer. It tends to be practiced in service-sales markets that have service regulatory requirements mandated by outside agencies. Rather than utilize their professional selling skills, they default to others. Typically their presentation strategies are focused on the words *requirement* or *codes*. Usually they're preceded by *state, JCAHO, FAA, fire marshal, city,* or some other agency name.

The mistake is assuming clients will do what is required. Salespeople also underestimate the possibilities that clients may contact other service providers who aren't trying to jam service agreements down their throats. Assuming you have the order in the sales profession isn't usually an attribute for long-term sales success.

Social

It's said that friends buy from friends. I'm not sure who said it, but for the most part I don't believe it. This presentation style assumes the salesperson has established a rapport with the client from a previous meeting and relies on that interaction to carry over to the presentation. In some cases it's nothing more than picking up the conversation where it left off.

In the right situation this strategy works well. If the qualifying call was successful, the bond between the salesperson and the client can be significant. Good salespeople build trust that can make their jobs easier. At the same time, when the discussion ultimately leads to addressing cost, things can change. Social bonds and money don't usually mix well. Business becomes business. People can like the same teams and have the same political views. It may be quite a coincidence that both of their mothers are named Margaret and both drive Audis. In the end it usually comes down to the value proposition being presented. Business is business.

Apologetic

There is nothing wrong with apologizing for being discourteous or for making an error that impacts another person. I have a long history of apologies for both of these reasons and others, but if I mentioned them I may have to apologize to you. I've watched a number of service salespeople who rely too heavily on this approach. In most cases I felt I was owed an apology for having to participate.

"I'm sorry I didn't get back to you sooner."

"I apologize for being three minutes late."

"I appreciate your time for meeting with me today."

"I'm sorry to see your plant is dying."

Individually any of these statements is fine. Typically more than one is pushing the oversensitive button too hard. Without any question the most detestable apology is, "I'm sorry we have to charge you so much." I've seen this happen and, not surprisingly, it turns my stomach. A service salesperson is the face of the company he represents. Some people may respond to this humble approach. Others may read it as a symptom of an ailing service provider.

Hit and Run

I'm stretching to call this a presentation style. It's the best moniker I could come up with for presentations that are more tragic events than controlled sales situations. Sometimes they are the results of poor scheduling or time management. Typically the salesperson or the client hasn't allotted enough time to conduct the meeting. The "clock is ticking" mentality pervades. If it's the result of a client issue, the best alternative is to attempt to reschedule the event. If it's due to poor planning on the service salesperson's part, the best alternative may be to enroll in a time-management course.

There's also a class of salespeople who don't enjoy or don't see the value in conducting sales presentations. I've seen great salespeople who are flawless qualifiers and who put their hearts and souls into every proposal drop the ball during presentations. I'm not sure if it's a case of stage fright or a lack of skills. It's painful to watch, knowing all the time and effort that went into preparing for this step in the sales cycle was probably wasted.

I've addressed styles used for presentations. Now let's look at methods. For the sake of argument I could have reversed the labels. The difference is how you present yourself (style) versus how you present the proposal (method). In this section I'm speaking about presenting the information.

We all have our own communication styles. Most presentation methods also track closely with our social styles. Expressive people like to talk, drivers like to be concise and get to the point, analytical people are always trying to figure things out, and the amiable are just nice people. We are who we are, but in a sales situation we may need to adjust our approaches, especially when presenting proposals. Listed below are common presentation styles.

- Narrative: This is the most common approach in a presentation setting. The sales person explains the proposal in story like fashion. It follows a logical format that helps the client understand what is being presented. In most cases it's effective, with a few exceptions.

   The first and most common error is covering too much detail. It takes time to present detailed information. It also opens the door for potential discussions of every detail, which can derail the presentation. One small detail can distract the client and submarine an otherwise great presentation.

   Other situations where narrative style may not work is when time is limited or the client has analytical or driver tendencies. As an analytical driver I'm of the cut-to-the-chase mode. No time for small talk; time is valuable; let's get to the point. The best alternative is usually an adaptation that presents the proposal in a narrative fashion but limits the level of detail. Typically this is done on the fly, as the client usually sets the tone of the meeting.

- Summary. Rather than focus on details, the summary method presents the key information: a simple overview of the services in the agreement, the benefits to be received, and the cost, and "here's where you sign." It works best when the services being proposed are simple to understand and the value proposition is clear.

  In contrast to the narrative style, care needs to be taken with a summary presentation being too brief. Most clients like to feel they are important and are entitled to being sold. A hasty service salesperson can make a big mistake by speeding through a proposal and not taking the time needed to convey the information. This is a case of balancing the time allowed for the presentation and covering the pertinent information.

- Back to front. This is a term I've used for many years. It's rooted in a service agreement design I developed that has a page at the end of the proposal that allows for crafting some special provisions for each client. In most cases they're not unique but presented in a way that looks customized for the client.

  Even if your service agreement doesn't allow this type of input, you can present the information orally or in your correspondence. This style attempts to quickly solicit a positive response from the client and demonstrates the professionalism of the salesperson. Rather than start the presentation with the boilerplate first page, i.e. price, it starts the meeting on a positive note. The salesperson reaffirms the special needs of the client rather than the standard services offered in the agreement.

Obviously it's important to have accuracy in what is highlighted. Affirming its Mr. Ciccotelli we need to call to schedule any service calls when it's actually Ms. Ciccotelli won't impress anyone. Noting all client calls will be handled as a priority and then listing various response-time levels is a contradiction. Another way of interpreting back to front is focusing on the client's perceived needs and benefits rather than the norm for similar clients. It's a client-centric approach, not customer-centric.

Presentation Tips

1. Practice. It's an obvious suggestion for others, but you probably don't need to practice. Yes, I'm being sarcastic. We all need to hone our skills. Admit it: you've either sat across from a client or spoken with one on the phone when you hadn't given any thought to the proposal until that moment. We all get too comfortable with our skills at some point in time.

    Practice doesn't require standing in front of a group of people and presenting your proposal, although that's not a bad idea. It means running the presentation through your mind beforehand. It may be as you travel to the call or while sitting in a waiting area at the client's office. There's nothing worse than not knowing the answer when a client asks a question about the proposal, especially when it's clearly notated. It doesn't send a great message when you're sitting there searching through the agreement for information you should have known. Practice doesn't always mean perfect, but it usually means you'll increase your income.

2. Multiple copies. I recommend presenting the client with two copies of the original proposal. Keep a photocopy

for your use and reference during the call. I don't suggest this because I believe the client will sign one original and keep one for his needs. That may happen on a few occasions, but it's not the norm. I do it because the majority of service agreements are reviewed by multiple people before a decision is made. I prefer to control the quality of the product, i.e. the proposal. I don't want someone distributing a copy that may be crooked, of inferior print quality, on cheap paper, or in black and white when I use a color logo. Hopefully the client will send one of the originals to whoever needs to review it.

3. Patience. We need to remember the client is seeing the proposal for the first time. Handing him the proposal while speaking at a speed typically brought on by too much coffee isn't the right approach. Hand the client your proposal package and wait for him to orientate himself. You shouldn't speak, speak, speak, speak and then pause. You should speak, pause, speak, pause, and allow the client some time to read and listen. Sometimes this requires quickly changing gears if you arrive late for the call and you're still operating at the high speed you were driving to reach the client. Take some breaths, compose yourself, and allow the client time to digest what he's seeing and hearing.

4. Observe the client. Watching the client's physical cues is important. Is he relaxed and listening? Is he distracted or glancing at his watch? Does he seem agitated before you even get started? Body language can tell us a lot about the client's level of interest and disposition. Interested clients welcome the meeting and are anxious to review the proposal. Distracted clients welcome you like you're the IRS. They give you that "what are you doing here?" look. If that's the case it may be best to reschedule.

The most important moment in the presentation is often overlooked by many good service salespeople. That's the moment when the client searches and locates the cost of the agreement. That usually occurs as soon as you hand him the proposal. Unless the client is a zombie, there will be some facial expression. A simple raise of an eyebrow can signify a good or bad level of surprise. A grin can say "this isn't as bad as I thought it would be." Gasping for breath isn't a good sign. The point is to focus on the client at that moment. I've been on too many calls where the salesperson is searching for a pen or looking away at that key moment. That initial facial expression is a great indicator of how the call will proceed and how much sales effort may be required.

5. Be confident in what you're selling. A service salesperson is an expert at crafting service proposals. That is implied with the position and should come across during the presentation. This is not the time and place to say "I think this is what you need" or "my best guess is this is the right solution." There's no room for comments like "I did a pretty good survey" or "hopefully this agreement should meet your needs."

    If the service salesperson conveys doubt in what she's proposing it will be evident to the client. This becomes very important when proposing to replace an existing service provider. Changing providers comes with a certain level of risk for clients. They need to feel confident that making the change will not put them in jeopardy. Confidence doesn't mean cocky. It means you're confident what you're proposing is what the client needs.

6. Don't oversell. Selling service is consultative by nature. It shouldn't require a hard sell. Repeatedly telling the client how good your company performs is usually a sign

of inadequacy or a lack of confidence. As previously mentioned I don't believe in only selling benefits. I prefer to enlighten clients about their service needs and how the proposal is the solution. Focus on the proposal and the client's needs.

Some salespeople can't stop themselves. They find themselves saying things like:

"You'll sleep better knowing you're covered."

"I've given you a great price."

"We may be higher priced than what you're paying now, but we're better."

Concerns in this area are the primary reason I'm not big on hiring people who have sold used cars. Most people respond positively to presentations that are honest and sincere representations of the service provider and their capabilities.

7. Shut up! This is somewhat related to *don't oversell*. I vividly recall, as does he, the first time I spent a day making sales calls with Greg Scott. He was one of the first people I hired at Simplex. It was Greg's first professional sales position. We spent the better part of a day making sales calls around Boston shortly after he attended my training class.

Throughout the day I kept my comments to a minimum as he was doing a good job. Greg has tremendous communication skills and an uncanny ability to read people. He had one obvious flaw that was evident during the calls. I knew I would have to say something special to make my point.

After a long day it was time for me to depart. He was anxious for some feedback. As I got in my car to leave I looked at him and said, "Learn to shut the hell up," and drove off. It may sound cruel, but that was what actually happened.

Greg has often told me how bad he felt and how he went home and told his wife, Nancy, about his bad review. At the same time he understood what I meant, and it made an impact. Greg went on to become one of my closest friends and one of the most successful service salespeople I've ever known. He also became my national service sales manager. It's not easy for expressive people to withstand times when no words are spoken. They feel the need to drown out the silence with chatter. However, quantity doesn't always mean quality.

I spoke about the goal of the presentation being the attainment of the order. Let's look at the impact of the presentation and the part it plays in the sales cycle. This requires another mediocre analogy.

You're an actor. You've honed your skills over the years to master your craft. You've weathered numerous tryouts and you got the part. Rehearsals go on for weeks as costumes, staging, and timing all come together. It's opening night. As expected you're nervous but confident. The curtain rises, the curtain falls, and you congregate with cast members and congratulate each other on your performances. In reality you knew fifteen minutes into the show you were bad and the reviews would kill you.

Somewhere in there is an analogy that applies to a person selling service. It takes skill and effort to identify prospects, qualify them, and prepare proposals. It can all go up in smoke if the presentation is anything less than curtain-call worthy.

Chapter 11

CLOSING
EASIER DONE THAN SAID

Closing is the most discussed step in the sales cycle. Countless books have been written on this specific topic. They include titles with descriptors like *secrets of*, *the art of*, *surefire*, and *master*. I've never read any of them. I've always felt this subject has been overdramatized. In all honesty the image that comes to mind when I see these books isn't good.

It was this type of subject matter that contributed to my not considering sales as a career. In my mind closing was a manipulative trick smooth talkers performed on innocent rubes. It was one of the reasons I held salesmen in contempt. I'd observed their bad behavior many times. There was the maudlin guy who sold my mom insurance while I was watching cartoons one Saturday morning. I remember what happened after my dad bought a used Pontiac from a pushy guy. Its transmission blew a few months later and caused some significant financial strain on my parents. I can't forget the guys in Western movies who would roll into town and sell tonics to a bunch of fools. I realize that wasn't actually closing but selling. Regardless, I didn't like it.

My impression didn't change much once I became a successful salesperson. I never liked to hear people refer to someone, especially me, as a "great closer." I don't consider myself a great closer. I consider myself a good salesperson. Closer references made me feel like my other sales skills were insignificant. Closing sales was not my only secret to success. I also didn't like to be grouped with others I knew had questionable sales skills but somehow closed a lot of sales.

I think my perspective on closing is best defined when analyzing the word. It can be used as a verb, noun, adjective, and adverb.

Close: This is the most common use of the word from my perspective. I used it constantly when working with salespeople. It was utilized two ways: "Did you close the proposal?" or "What is your close rate?" These very simple questions would often turn into discussions or contentious debates.

Let's look at the first one. Did you close the proposal? In my mind there are only two answers: "yes" or "no." A proposal is either sold or not sold. *Close* doesn't mean giving a great presentation, client's promising to purchase, or the ever-popular "I feel good about it." It simply means did you get the order? Is it booked? You can forecast a sale, but it's still not closed.

As for *close rate*, it's a simple math question. Divide sales by quotes and you get a close rate. This question would often generate a blank "I should know this" look or a diversionary ploy—a battery of questions that had obvious answers, at least from my perspective:

"Do you mean all of my proposals or just the ones I really thought I could sell?"

"What do I do if I give a customer multiple proposals on the same system?"

"Do I mix bids and negotiated sales together?"

"Do I count proposals that won't be decided on for a few months?"

It's simple. A proposal is a proposal and a sale is a sale.

Closer: Recently it's been the title of a popular television show in which Kyra Sedgwick closes cases by eliciting confessions or cornering suspects through sometimes-questionable methods.

Here *closer* is used in a way that doesn't reflect the word in a favorable light. The character's skill is the art of manipulation.

If you're a baseball fan you also know the closer is the pitcher who comes in the last inning to get the last three outs. It's common knowledge by followers of the game that closers are typically a little weird.

In sales a closer is the person known for bringing in sales. There's nothing wrong with that, but it oversimplifies the array of skills required to be a successful salesperson.

Closing: This is the title of this chapter for a reason. I don't see closing as an event that occurs at the end of the presentation. Closing is the end result of a process. It's the natural act that occurs if the sales job is done well. Most overachieving service salespeople are heavy on relationships and light on the close. For these individuals closing the sale is easy, as most of the heavy lifting was done in the previous steps in the sales cycle. For many underachievers it's the step in the sales cycle when they think they are defeated. That's rarely the case, though. They were probably defeated days or weeks earlier. Still, they tend to judge their overall sales performance on this one measurement.

Weak sales managers may do the same. Good sales managers are more concerned with finding out why the proposal didn't close. In many cases sales are lost when salespeople choose to prospect in market segments that have too much competition. They lose sales when they don't qualify the prospect properly. They lose sales when they propose solutions that don't meet the needs of their clients. They lose sales when they act arrogant with their clients' associates or send poorly worded e-mails. I could go on, but I think you get the point.

A good salesperson is closing the order from their first contact with the client. Every communication, written or verbal, is part of the closing process. The handshake, grooming and appearance, and tone of voice are all parts of the closing process. Good salespeople are always closing. They do it unconscientiously. It comes naturally to top performers. They're always on. They don't need to put special emphasis on the closing call or learn tricks from master closers. They know closing is the result of a being a professional salesperson every step of the way.

Service Sale Versus Product Sale

Similar to other steps in the sales cycle, closing service sales presents different issues and opportunities versus product sales. At Honeywell it was not uncommon to take a prospect to a current client to see a system in operation. The prospect would gain a sense of how the system performed and interact with one of our customers. These site visits usually had significant impacts on closing sales. The clients felt reassurance in knowing our claims of energy savings were substantiated by actual users of our equipment.

Sometimes we flew clients to Chicago to visit our customer center. It was an impressive facility attached to our factory in Arlington Heights. These well-choreographed demonstrations impressed every prospect and our own salespeople. I bet at least 75 percent of these clients ended up purchasing systems.

Factory tours, demonstrations, site visits, and even samples are commonly used as closing tools in technical-product and system sales. In the case of service, these types of experiences are limited. The most common sales tool available is providing some current customers the prospect can contact for references. Unlike a demonstration or tour that is controlled by the salesperson, this tactic presents its own risks. Sometimes references can make innocent comments to prospects that do more harm than good. In almost all cases these comments start with the phrase "they're a good company to work with, but..." I could fill in the blank with numerous comments that had me on the defense when I followed up with my prospects. Usually they were solvable, but in some cases references worked against me.

I always caution people to work closely with their references to ensure they're prepared to take calls from prospects. As mentioned earlier service performance perceptions can change on any given day. A client can be happy one day and the next day be frustrated and upset. There's always a chance the prospect could contact the customer on that off day.

Some service salespeople use technical staff as sales aids. They introduce technicians to prospective clients, attempting to make the service more tangible. This tactic can be helpful given the right circumstances. I recall doing this once and finding myself waiting in my client's office for over an hour—the technician arrived late for our meeting. Obviously this didn't go the way I had planned. I did my best tap dance to cover my embarrassment. I was always supported by great technicians, but in all honesty I would be on the edge of my seat with each word they spoke to my client. The vast majority of the meetings went well. On the occasions they didn't, it usually cost me the sale.

On the positive side, service sales presents some unique circumstances that aren't common when selling systems or products. The clients already have the equipment we're trying to sell service agreements on. They've already made the big-dollar investments to buy it. We're providing service to protect their investments. In some cases the equipment is already in need of repair or is operating at less-than-peak efficiency. We don't need to demo anything. We can usually point out something that's broken or in need of maintenance.

Our best testimonial may be a comment from an unhappy tenant or user of the equipment in need of service that finds its way to the client. A reference to a code or an official may be a testimonial that the client doesn't want to hear, but we may slip it into the conversation. Closing a service sale is reality based. It's not about bells, whistles, or shiny, new things. It's about keeping those things shiny and new as long as possible.

Trial Close

The trial close is a common selling technique. The salesperson asks a question that tests the prospect's reaction. These questions usually give the salesperson insight into how the client is feeling about the purchase. It's a great way to uncover information that can be used to adjust the conversation moving forward.

Typically good trial close questions are poised to generate positive responses rather than answers that put the sale in a "yes" or "no" position:

- Would you prefer we do our maintenance tasks in the morning or afternoon?
- Who would you like us to contact when our technician arrives?
- What do you think of our documentation? (Assuming it's good.)
- Which of the services I'm proposing is most important to you?
- Would you prefer us to contact you by phone or e-mail to schedule our inspections?
- Would you be available to attend our free users' conference in Hawaii?

Trial close questions allow prospects to express their feelings and help build trusting relationships. They present minimal risk as long as the questions don't challenge the clients or put them in positions where they can reject the proposals.

Trial closing questions should be used throughout the sales cycle, not just during the closing call. In reality the best time to pose trial close questions is during the qualifying call.

They're a great way to gain important insight and information about the client and uncover any issues that may need to be solved before a proposal is created. If done correctly the closing call becomes the logical outcome of the trial close questions.

Closing Argument

We've all watched or read dramatic closing arguments at fictitious trials. They are the concluding statements for trials that could have lasted days, weeks, or even months. Attorneys present evidence in a manner that will best represent their clients with the hope of persuading the jury or judge to make decisions in their favor. Trial closing arguments are crafted to generate the right answer: guilty or not guilty. It's "has the jury reached a decision?" time. Everyone takes a deep breath and the outcome is determined.

"Your honor, the jury has found the proposal to contain the solutions that are needed, and we have decided to make the purchase." The lawyer and client shake hands, and happiness reigns for the winner. As for the losers, it's much the opposite. They feel the shock of reality and suffer the consequences of defeat.

Every salesperson has been on both sides of the decision. Making a sale is a joyful experience; getting rejected sucks. Evading the question will not resolve the situation. It's time to ask for the order.

For many salespeople the most or least enjoyed moment in the sales cycle is asking for the order. Some prolong the event by dancing around the question, hoping the prospect will tell them they have the order without their asking. I for one have had issues in this area. I didn't fear asking for my prospects' business. I feared rejection. Nobody enjoys rejection. It's hard to accept all the effort you've put into something resulting in failure.

However, in sales, failure is not an optional experience. It's standard equipment. It comes with the job. Some people convince themselves they've asked for the order, but in reality they've only alluded to it. Hearing positive responses to questions isn't asking for the order.

Sometimes you don't have to ask. There were many occasions when the client was receptive to the presentation and told me the proposal looked good and picked up the phone to call purchasing for a PO number. The best-case scenario is when the client signs the proposal on the spot. Good salespeople go into a closing call visualizing getting the signature and driving away with the sale in hand. Unfortunately this is a fairly rare occurrence in today's service sales environment. More often than not, paperwork needs to be processed or aspects of the agreement need to be reviewed by people within the client's organization. Regardless it's a good mental exercise and motivational tool to pump you up before a closing call.

It's time to ask for the business. You sense the moment is right. The client also seems to realize this is the point in the call when resolution in needed. What do you say? How do you position the question without seeming pushy or insensitive? Sooner or later all the trial close questions are answered and you need to ask the final question. I've observed many salespeople asking for the order. I still ask people I'm training how they handle it. Their answers—the questions they ask—have remained constant over the years:

- When can we schedule our first service call?
- What start date would you like me to put on the agreement?
- Can I have your signature or a purchase order number?

These are good questions that should solicit responses. Sometimes the answer will be a simple "yes" or "no." Other times a question or objection may be raised. All too commonly the client will make the dreaded "let me think about it" comment. Most experienced salespeople have their own styles and approaches to closing sales. I have mine, which has served me well over the years. I used it as a salesperson and I continue to use it as a consultant. In almost all cases it either provides resolution or opens the door for additional conversation and the opportunity to resell the proposal.

A common activity for all service providers, regardless of the product or system that requires service, is scheduling. Sooner or later a technician will need to be scheduled to visit the site to perform service. It may be for general maintenance, repair, testing, or an inspection. In the best cases the client needs immediate repair. In all situations scheduling is involved.

Some service providers require advance notice of a day or two. Others can extend into weeks as calendars get crowded. If extensive travel is required, a technician visit may need to be coordinated with other clients in the geographical area. The schedule card is the wild card. It can be played how you want to play it. Some salespeople make reference to the fact that their service staff is very busy and advance scheduling will be needed, so approving the proposal immediately will help expedite the call. Others promise to provide quick scheduling to entice the client to sign. Both are good tactics, but in my mind too passive.

I played the schedule card in a fashion that made my clients feel like I was their advocate. I took a proactive stance that demonstrated my commitment to serving them. In all honesty my tactic had nothing to do with these perceptions. My motive was self-centered. First I needed to know if I was getting their business that day. Tomorrow was too far away. Calling them back in a week was an eternity. I needed to know now. I wanted to be in a position to tell my manager the status of the business, with certainty, right after the meeting. Secondary was my desire to resolve any outstanding issues while I was with clients. Most of my service agreements weren't large enough to warrant return visits. If the clients had concerns that hadn't been uncovered, I couldn't walk away without addressing them.

My goal was clear: I needed to know at the closing call if I was getting the order. I needed one last shot to answer any issues that may have been overlooked. I needed to know if I hadn't properly qualified the prospect in the first place. If that were the case I had the opportunity to start re-qualifying the client on the spot. To accomplish this I took a proactive, assumptive position. If the client hadn't voluntarily given me approval I used my best closing tactic: "Mr. Involuntary, I've taken the liberty of scheduling your service for Monday, April eleventh. If you can give me the go-ahead today I'll be able to confirm that date."

This statement always triggered a response. I wasn't asking a question. I wasn't implying something. It was plain and simple. I wanted the client to visualize a service vehicle pulling up to his door on the eleventh of April. There was no other way to interpret it. Rather than waiting for approval to *start* the service agreement, they had to *stop* me. My strategy was proactive. I was taking action and they needed to respond. Typically I received one of the following three responses:

1. "That sounds good. I'll let my people know you'll be coming on the eleventh." Obviously this was the best-case scenario. They would give me verbal approval, sign the proposal, or contact purchasing to process the order. These individuals were properly qualified, were receptive to my service value proposition, and were ready to move forward. I estimate this was the response a third of the time.

2. "Hold that date, but I'll need to get back to you later in the week." Not as definitive as number one, but the probability of closing the deal was good. In the majority of cases, the prospect needed to verify something before moving forward. It could be as simple as confirming something with purchasing or passing the proposal by someone else for a sanity check. In the majority of cases, I'd receive an approval within a week. Of course I'd make every effort to schedule the follow-up call when I was in front of the client. A generic "I'll get back to you" wasn't acceptable. I estimate this was the response about 20 percent of the time.

3. "Hold on. I'm not ready to make a decision. I need to think about this." This was the most common response. I probably heard it in one form or another about half the time. It wasn't as good as getting the approval, but it had its own merits. It's an honest response. There's a reason why the client was being hesitant. Did he really need time to think? Was there something in the proposal that confused him or that he didn't see the value in? Was he going to get a proposal from another vendor to compare? These were all rational concerns.

My most troubling concerns were: Had I properly qualified him? Was he actually the decision maker? Did he have enough funding for my agreement? Whatever the scenario my statement generated a response that allowed me to explore the situation on the spot. Never did I just shake the client's hand and say, "Get back to me when you're ready." That was the easy way out for both of us.

I would always voice my surprise and ask him what in particular his concern was. I attempted to open up a dialogue right then and there. Often I was able to address the client's concern and receive the go-ahead. Many times it meant retracing my steps. That may have led to submitting a new proposal or uncovering that my client wasn't actually the decision maker. Whatever the case, I wasn't going to just ride off into the sunset.

My approach isn't a traditional closing technique. Then again I wasn't the typical service salesperson or I wouldn't have put myself in a position to have written this book. When it comes to closing service sales, there are six opportunities during the typical closing call:

- Summarize the offering, benefits, and price (ask for the order).

  It's simple and straightforward but doesn't usually go this smoothly. It allows the salesperson to present the proposal in a logical fashion. If the prospect has been properly qualified it has a high probability of success.
- Restate areas of the agreement; present a new benefit (ask for the order).

  Highlight an area in the agreement that targets a specific need or concern of the client. This tactic is most often used when the first option doesn't generate an affirmative response. It's often utilized multiple times during the same closing call. On occasion it borders on desperation if not controlled.
- Handle objections (ask for the order).

  I'll cover this important area in the next chapter.
- Present penalties for not buying (ask for the order).

  Caution! This doesn't mean threatening the client. Professional service salespeople do not do stupid ploys like warning of a price increase, noting how the client can rest better knowing he is covered by an agreement, or not giving non-service-agreement clients call priority.

These types of desperate moves almost always turn off the client. The best use of this tactic is outlined above. "If you can give me the go-ahead we'll be able to schedule a visit to your facility next Friday." Is there an implied penalty? Yes—the service call may be delayed. Is there a threat? No—the service call can be rescheduled.

- Reference (ask for the order).

    Providing references can be a tricky business. Not only do you risk having the client call them on a bad day, but you may provide a reference in competition with or held in disdain by your client. Many salespeople provide large key accounts as references during either the qualifying or closing call. They think name dropping will impress their clients. In some cases it works, while in others it can undermine the whole situation.

    Some people, like me, really don't care what the other guy is doing. I take pride in making independent decisions. For some name dropping triggers a feeling of being manipulated or even discredited. I think reference selling is best used when attempting to make the client more comfortable with a particular offering. A good example would be proposing an agreement that includes maintenance and parts to a client who has historically purchased only testing or time and material services. The client understands the concept but is struggling with the large increase in the price of the service agreement. In this case referencing a customer who saw her overall annual expenditures go down after purchasing an inclusive agreement may help. If it's a reference with a similar facility, that's even better. It's typically not a good idea to provide references when they're not requested unless you're a new service provider with a limited track record.

- Special concession (ask for the order).

Offering a discount isn't a special concession; it's just selling out. I'm speaking about offering the client something that appears to be outside the norm. Sometimes a minor detail can move a tentative decision maker to a "yes." Some common concessions are altering billing periods, expediting scheduling, special documentation, allowing the client's personnel to assist, or any other opportunity that presents itself. Resorting to offering a discount is not a special concession. It's recognition you could have done a better job.

Accepting Defeat

You can't win them all. Some great efforts go up in smoke. In most situations the reason for not closing the deal is identifiable. The client may make a demand that is difficult to meet or unreasonable. You may have done everything in your means to get the sale but the answer is still "no." It doesn't feel good. It's not uncommon to feel angry with the client. You may feel like you've been used and want to lash out verbally. It's not easy but you need to swallow your pride and take the high road. Thank the client for his time and move on. Burning bridges serves no purpose. There's a high probability the client will surface again, maybe at another location. It happens all the time.

Early in my career I know I dropped a few "you'll be sorry" type comments before departing from non-purchasing clients. I also know a large part of my sales came from repeat customers who had moved on to other facilities and contacted me. I can only wonder how may sales I may have gained if I hadn't burned some bridges. I've also sold many service agreements by circling back to prospects that chose other service providers. In almost all cases it was due to their lower prices. If I had burnt those bridges they may have gone elsewhere.

Closing rates in service sales are directly proportional to how well prospects are qualified. One of my most extensive studies examined close rates as they related to the quality of the qualification process. The sample included over 1,000 proposals both sold and unsold. I interviewed dozens of salespeople. All had lost proposals. I analyzed their sales based on the WFAN criteria.

For proposals that went unsold, the most commonly lacking qualification criterion was authority. Submitting a proposal to an individual who wasn't responsible for authorizing it resulted in half of all lost sales. Lack of willingness, funding, or need accounted for the other half of lost efforts. It was somewhat surprising that these three were almost equal in priority.

In many cases multiple criteria (WFA or N) had not been qualified properly. Needless to say very few of those turned into sales.

Most salespeople believe price is the most common reason for losing a sale. This study, and others, determined that's not usually the case. Closing success, for the most part, is determined during the first call. Submitting proposals to unqualified prospects isn't the path to becoming an overachieving service salesperson.

Chapter 12

OBJECTION HANDLING
HIT ME WITH YOUR BEST SHOT

Upon returning to my branch office after my Honeywell training debacle, I was given a reprieve by my sympathetic boss. He was confident I would prove the experts in Minneapolis wrong and become a successful service salesperson. I was assigned a desk and commenced organizing my workspace. I assembled the necessary paper, pens, pencils, message pads, customer files, and technical information. I had the most organized desk in the bullpen.

I decided it could be better, so I organized it again and again. After a few days of demonstrating my organization prowess, my boss, Ed Neary, strongly hinted it was time for me to go out and make calls. Prior to my training I'd made sales calls with other people in the office. It was time to go solo. I wasn't comfortable with that, but I had run out of procrastination excuses and it was time.

Not surprisingly I was anxious; the memory of my disastrous role play was hard to shake. I wasn't afraid of meeting new people or asking qualifying questions or doing surveys. I was afraid of clients' potential questions. In particular the questions I should know the answers to. I wasn't trained on what questions to expect or how to answer them. I had no problem being honest with clients and telling them I didn't know the answer to a technical question. I knew I could ask someone in my office that had a technical background for help. As mentioned above

I didn't know the questions, so responding with the correct answers was definitely going to be a challenge.

Handling objections is easy when you know in advance the most common objections and possible answers. In reality there aren't that many, so advanced preparation helps. Unfortunately many service salespeople aren't trained properly. They give inadequate responses and learn the hard way, typically at the cost of some lost sales.

First you need to understand the difference between a question and an objection. Questions are usually asked to obtain information or clarification. Objections usually mean there's some level of disapproval with something. Some salespeople make mistakes and handle questions like they are objections. The client asks a simple question and the salesperson gives an explanation or defends something that isn't necessary. "Can I have this invoiced quarterly?" It's a simple question. It should be answered in a few words and not like the following response: "It's our company policy to bill in advance. I can offer you special billing if you need it. By the way we can't do the first inspection until we receive payment."

Sometimes there may be an objection inside a simple question, but don't go down that path without reason. The best thing to do is answer the client's question and gauge their response. If there isn't a follow-up or comment, move on.

Objections can surface at any step in the sales cycle. I think they're more subliminal during the qualifying call and more in your face during the closing call. I'd much rather have objections come up during the first call than the last. One unsolved objection can undermine a sales effort. It's better to know any issues early on. It allows you to disqualify the prospect if an objection can't be resolved or take it into consideration when developing the offering and proposal.

I respect clients who ask difficult questions. I think they do it because it's what a good-conscience buyer should do.

They're doing what's expected. I strongly believe objections present opportunities. Clients who voice legitimate concerns demonstrate they have a level of interest in purchasing. I feel less confident with individuals who have no questions or objections. I'd be suspect of the person who tells you everything looks fine and he'll get back to you. That lack of interest usually doesn't translate into an order.

Interested parties ask questions and raise concerns. In many situations questions posed to service salespeople aren't generated by the people asking them. They may be asked for someone else in the organization. The client may also be anticipating questions that others may ask them.

Handling Objections

- Welcome the objection. It's normal to become defensive when someone raises an objection, but this is an absolute no-no in sales. Regardless of what issue is raised, react in a positive manner. That normally means responding with phrases like:

  "I see your point."

  "I understand why that would concern you."

  "That's a great point you're bringing up."

  These types of responses will help distill any negative feelings or emotions. They often disarm the person raising the objection and make him feel his concerns are legitimate and taken seriously.

- Listen closely. Sometimes there may be a question within the question, or the client is posing the objection in a confusing way. I often find myself finishing a client's question in my head, thinking I've heard it a million times before. This type of over-assurance can cost you if you don't listen to each question with care. I know I've made this mistake on many occasions due to impatience on my part. A simple inflection in the voice can alter the meaning of a question. Listening skills are essential in sales. They are tested when it comes to reading and interpreting objections.

- Show empathy. Always look at the objection from the client's point of view. What is the basis of this objection? Is she disappointed in what's being offered? Does she feel bad because she can't afford to purchase the service agreement? Has something occurred that has the client in a bad frame of mind? It's very important to show empathy for clients who make claims of being mistreated by your company. It doesn't matter what their complaints are. I always acknowledge them and convey I wouldn't have handled it as well as they did. This strategy normally turns a negative situation into a positive one.

- Don't personalize. Raising an objection about your company shouldn't be taken personally. For most of us that's not easy, as we're loyal to our employers. This can be very difficult for people who have been employed by the same firm for many years. In those cases it's hard to separate yourself from your company, but you have to.

  Most of us in sales have some level of self-centeredness in our personalities. We can internalize anything. I've watched salespeople whose physical demeanors immediately changed when negative comments were made about their companies. I could see them tighten up and take on defensive postures. It's one thing to be loyal, but remember it's a business meeting, not a debate.

- Seek clarification. This is an important tactic for two reasons. The first and most obvious is to make sure you understand the objection. Often, restating the objection to the client helps:

"I will not sign a multi-year agreement."

"Are you saying you'll approve this agreement if it's for only one year?"

This seems like a good answer, but maybe the client really means he doesn't have the authority to approve multi-year agreements, or he may be planning on replacing the equipment. It could be a number of different issues, so clarification is needed.

The other reason to ask for clarification is it can buy you time to create your answer. It never hurts to have a couple of minutes to review your response mentally before verbalizing it.

- Negotiate a win-win. An objection doesn't mean you have to respond in a way that always acquiesces to the client's wants and desires. Clients are free to make demands of any supplier. Some are rational and easy to resolve. Others may require special approval or challenge the operating policies of the service provider. In those cases the service salesperson has to be upfront and explain the issue to the client. A negotiation isn't a "my way or the highway" approach. Typically a solution that will appease the client and not compromise the values of the company or the service salesperson can be found somewhere in the middle.

- Answer the objection. It seems obvious, but it doesn't always happen. Admit it: you've heard an objection and smoothly changed the subject, hoping the client didn't notice. In all honesty that can happen, but it shouldn't if the salesperson takes a professional approach and handles the issue. It's not enough to agree and move on. The client may feel appeased at the moment, but that unanswered objection will usually surface later. In may be when the client decides he won't purchase the service agreement. At that point it's too late to backtrack as he may not give you the opportunity to revisit the situation.

- Practice. There are typically only a dozen or so objections in most service-sales markets. They tend to be similar regardless of the system or product that needs service. You've probably heard the same objections over and over again. With that said it's important not to respond to the client's concerns in a mechanical fashion. It can give the client the impression you're insincere or make her feel like her issues aren't important. Below I've listed the ten most common objections I've heard in person or from service salespeople I've trained across multiple industries.

1. The price is too high!

No doubt about it—this is the big one. It's the bane of every salesperson. Why does price ruin great sales opportunities? Sometimes it's subtle: "This isn't what I was expecting." Oftentimes it comes as a surprise: "I asked for a proposal from your competitor and their price is lower." Some clients respond like they're being punked: "Are you kidding me?" While others question your mental state: "Are you crazy?"

Price is the most common objection. I would estimate that it surfaces in over half of all service-sales situations. I also believe in half of those cases the objection is rhetorical. These individuals would object to the price if it were free. It's a natural purchasing response when any numbers are preceded by a dollar sign. Needless to say there are many situations when the price is too high. This is usually due to poorly qualifying the prospect in the first place. If there isn't enough funding available to purchase the service agreement then something was overlooked in the qualifying call.

The first step is not to panic. If you've created a service agreement that contains a package of offerings, you should be able to justify it or offer to reduce the coverage to bring down the price. If you've presented a service agreement that's standard and can be offered by other service providers, that's a different situation. It's hard to overcome the price objection when you're selling a commodity. It's much easier to justify price when an apples-to-apples comparison isn't the case. If the prospect can reach into a drawer and pull out the same offering from a competitor and it's a lower price, good luck. You can sell your firm's value proposition if there's some differentiation that gives you an edge. If not, it's time to rethink your sales strategy as this scenario will repeat itself if nothing changes.

2. Let me think about it.

On the surface this common refrain doesn't appear to fit in the objection-handling category. The client isn't raising an objection or asking a question. I think most people take some time to think things over before making important decisions. I don't think there's a surefire way to turn this response into a "yes." Once someone makes this statement there isn't much that can be done to change their mind. I don't think challenging statements like "what do you need to think about?" or "don't you want to get started right away?" will turn many people around. You can try to change the client's mind, but for the most part the best thing to do is schedule the follow-up call and hope for the best. Hopefully he will agree. Worst case, he'll tell you he'll contact you when he's made a decision.

You're left hanging, the proposal is in jeopardy, and the probability of closing the deal took a sharp turn for the worse. But it's easy to tell yourself otherwise and hope for the best as you drive away. The best way to minimize putting yourself into this situation may be a proactive tactic like saying, "I've taken the liberty of scheduling the inspection," which I outlined earlier. It worked for me.

3. Thanks for the proposal, but I'll just call when I need service.

This may be the most frustrating objection of all. You've done a good job of qualifying the prospect and developing an offer that meets her needs. You enlightened the prospect and she agreed the work needs to be done. Based on your sales interaction she will most likely call your company when she needs service. She appears to like you and your firm. The cost of the proposal didn't seem to be an issue. But she wouldn't approve it.

Most salespeople's first thoughts are the lost incentive dollars and quota attainment. My initial response would be surprise, followed closely by disappointment. In some cases salespeople receive compensation for generating time and material revenue, but that's not always the case. Either way this response isn't acceptable. It's time to re-qualify the client. That's assuming she was qualified in the first place.

I think for the most part this response is the result of submitting a proposal for a service agreement to someone who really didn't have the willingness to purchase one in the first place. Funding, authority, and need garner most of the attention during the qualifying phase. The most often overlooked criterion is willingness. Too many salespeople are too willing to submit proposals to prospects who aren't interested. If you're hearing this objection often, that's a problem.

4. I don't have this much money in my budget.

I could take the easy way out and point to poor qualifying once again. Clearly there's a funding issue. The first thing to do is establish with the client that the service agreement contains the right offering to meet his needs. If he agrees the proposal isn't the issue and the budget is the only barrier, there's hope.

A cooperative client will usually welcome a discussion about options like spreading out payments. The salesperson can also offer to change the effective date to coincide with the client's budget year. Is there a possibility to combine funds from two budget areas? The important thing is to cement your partnership with the client and show your intent to work with him to solve the problem.

This objection is more common during difficult economic times, as budget cutting becomes the norm. Showing your empathy for the client's situation can go a long way. If it's simply a case of no funding options being available, then it's another case of improperly qualifying the prospect.

5. This proposal looks good. I'll have to run it by my boss.

Hopefully, by this point in the book, you understand submitting proposals to sponsors, and not decision makers, isn't a good idea. Yes, there are occasions when the authority figure is inaccessible or will not meet with you. I understand the proposal will be authorized in Fargo, North Dakota, and you're located in Lancaster, Pennsylvania. I know it may tick off your sponsor if you go over his head, especially when he's the one who contacted you in the first place. Without him you wouldn't even be there.

I get it. I understand, but I still don't buy it. You need to make every attempt to meet, speak with, or electronically communicate with the person who will authorize the service agreement. There will be many exceptions. A sponsor is often emphatic when telling you he needs to run the proposal by his boss. I don't want my proposal *running by* anyone. I want the boss to take the time to read and understand it. I want her to interface with me so I can answer any questions or objections. It's one thing to know you're not meeting with the authorizing party. If you thought your client was the decision maker and you hear this statement during the closing call, it's clearly a failure on your part.

6. Why do I have to pay for a service agreement in advance?

Unlike with a product, there's little recourse when service is purchased, performed, and not paid for. This objection is rarely raised with most service providers as they operate in a prepay environment as a business policy. Inside staff, sales personnel, technicians, and customers are well aware of the fact. Most companies don't require prepay for time and material work, but some will ask for purchase order numbers. The majority will process, invoice, and wait for payment before performing services as part of a service agreement. This is particularly the case when the client is new and has no track record with the provider.

Over the years I've been surprised by how many companies didn't require prepay. I wasn't surprised many of those companies also had receivables issues. What was most troubling was they never even asked for prepay when similar providers were doing otherwise. Not only did those other providers have less receivables issues, but they also had better cash flow.

The answer to the client isn't about policy or a lack of trust. It's about economics. The correct response is explaining to the client the proposal is based on an annual invoice paid in advance. If he would like to be invoiced quarterly or even monthly, you will need to get approval and a finance charge will be added. As for doing work in advance of payment, that's a business decision service providers need to make. In my opinion it should be the exception, not the rule.

In the majority of cases clients will agree to prepay. In cases where they don't agree, special considerations may be necessary. The role the service salesperson plays is critical. One of the primary parts of the service-sales compensation plans I design is paying the salesperson their incentive upon invoicing. Not surprisingly salespeople do great jobs of handling this objection when it affects their personnel incomes. They obviously prefer to receive their incentive immediately, rather than over time.

7. I worked with your company before and I wasn't impressed.

This comment typically surfaces when trying to schedule a first call or during the qualifying call. It can also occur during the closing call if the client invites someone new to the meeting. Unless you were the perpetrator of the client's issue, this objection can usually be turned into a positive situation. You need to practice some basic disciplines. Listen with interest, be empathetic, and don't take it personally. No matter what the issue, the answer should be the same:

- "I'm surprised to hear about your problem."
- "I understand why you were upset."
- "Let me tell you some of the things we've done to improve our performance."

If you're a new, dedicated service salesperson for a company that hasn't previously had the position, you've got the perfect answer: "I understand we've had some issues in the past. The company has taken some steps to improve our service delivery. I'm part of the solution as we now have people, like me, whose sole responsibility is meeting with our customers to ensure we provide the right service solutions to meet their needs." It's a win for the company. It's a win for the salesperson. It's a win for the client because he was heard, no excuses were provided, and part of the solution is in front of him.

8. I think my own people can do some of this work.

This objection can be a little tricky. The first step is quickly recalling information obtained during the qualifying call, assuming one took place. If the closing call is the only call it can be more challenging.

Clearly the issue is the client's staff availability and training. Is there trained staff available to perform the needed service? And are they licensed, if that's a requirement? In most cases the answer is "no." The problem becomes how to work your way tactfully through the issue. You don't want to challenge the client and imply she doesn't have the smarts to do the work. It's also not a good idea to ask if the client has in-house capabilities, why hasn't maintenance been performed.

I find my best tactic is congratulating the client on having trained staff to perform the work, as most of my other clients are stretched due to reductions in manpower. This usually starts the client's gears turning around the reality of the situation. She needs help or she wouldn't have agreed to see you in the first place.

I think the primary issue behind this objection is budgetary. Typically the client is looking for a financial solution. She wants to purchase the services needed but can't afford it. Some firms will offer solutions that allow clients' staff to assist the service provider's technician. Sometimes there can be a savings by both parties. Unfortunately, all too often, the person assigned to assist just slows down the service delivery.

In most cases this objection opens up a conversation that, if handled correctly, leads to a sale. For people who sell service agreements on highly technical equipment, this objection is rare, as their clients have limited options.

9. Your company doesn't have enough experience with (fill in the blank).

This objection is most common for service providers who are extending their brands. By that I mean providing services on equipment or systems they don't install or have limited track records on. Common client concerns are issues related to servicing another manufacturer's equipment, the experience level of technicians, the type or size of the client's facility, managing subcontracts, or the age of the company. These are all justifiable concerns.

The best approach is to explain the processes involved to support the delivery of the service. This may include information on parts or software sourcing, manufacturer support, or detail on the training and skills of the technicians who will support the account. A common tactic is providing the client with a direct number for someone with management responsibilities if the client purchases an agreement. This often gives the reassurance the client is looking for.

If the major concern is the size or age of the service provider it must be dealt with honestly: "Yes, we're a new company, but we're committed to providing you with the best service available. We take pride in being responsive and building personnel relationships with each of our customers." In most cases these clients are speaking with new service providers because their current providers aren't getting the job done or are charging too much. Typically they want the new provider to succeed as much as the service company wants to succeed.

10. Thanks for the proposal. I've decided to put the work out for bid.

I've saved my least favorite for last. If you've ever heard this objection you've probably felt surprised and very likely suppressed anger. If this is reality and not some ploy by the client to manipulate you, it's not a good situation.

The occasions when I've been in this position made me feel like I'd been used. In reality that was what happened. A client used my expertise to help build a great service specification. Rather than trying to create one, he sought someone out to do the work for him. Typically this situation happens to salespeople who represent manufacturers, as they have access to professional service specifications and procedures.

Once again the problem appears to be related to poor qualification of the client. Typically that's not the case with this objection. Rarely do clients change their purchasing strategies at this point in the sales cycle. They probably had this card up their sleeves from the start. Yes, you were deceived. The best you can do is try to understand why the work will go out for bid and if there is any way you can gain a competitive edge. Typically it doesn't go well, as your price has been exposed. The primary question is, do you continue to work with this client or walk away? I limit myself to playing the fool a maximum of one time per client.

ABOUT THE AUTHOR

Joe Siderowicz has more than twenty-five years of experience in service marketing. He has interviewed, hired, trained, or mentored more than 5,000 service salespeople. He is a recognized leader in his field, having built and led multiple worldwide service organizations.

Mr. Siderowicz has held executive sales, marketing, and general management positions with the industry-leading companies Honeywell and Simplex. He is the founder and president of the AfterMarket Consulting Group, which advises companies on how to grow service revenue. His extensive client list includes Fortune 100 firms and independent companies both large and small.

Mr. Siderowicz has extensive public-speaking experience with large corporate, convention, and trade-show groups. He has contributed articles on service sales and service marketing to numerous publications.

A graduate of Temple University and the University of Pennsylvania's Wharton School, Mr. Siderowicz resides with his wife in suburban Boston, Massachusetts.

CPSIA information can be obtained
at www.ICGtesting.com
Printed in the USA
LVOW04s0230211216
518200LV00007B/140/P